Secret of the Twelve Stones

Secret of the Twelve Stones

The Journey to Presence

Colin P. Sisson

Waterside Press

Copyright ©2018 by Colin P. Sisson

All rights reserved. This book or any portion thereof may not be reproduced or used in any manner whatsoever without the express written permission of the publisher except for the use of brief quotations in a book review.

Printed in the United States of America

First Printing, 2018

ISBN-13: 978-1-939116-80-2 print edition
ISBN-13: 978-1-939116-81-9 ebook edition

Waterside Publishing
2055 Oxford Ave
Cardiff, CA 92007
www.waterside.com

Acknowledgements

MAGDALENA JANICKA
I want to express my deep gratitude and love to Magdalena for her contribution to this book. Not only as my first proof reader, but also many of the ideas expressed in this book were inspired by her.

MICHAEL FREEDMAN – My most important spiritual teacher, something I discovered after many years after his passing. He was my first introduction to the practice of being present. I will be forever grateful to him.

MIRIAM RUBERL – Who completed the main proof reading and editing of this edition and made it more readable. Thank you.

OSHO – A great thank you for his inspiration of the two journeys home, intellect and intuition.

FRANK HERBERT – for a quote from his book, Dune – about the passage of fear.

PAMELA WADE – Who completed the final proof reading and editing of this edition. Thank you.

Contents

Chapter	Page
Getting the most out of this book	ix
Foreword	xi
1. The Map	1
2. The adventure begins	10
3. Harold's horror	16
4. River crossing	22
5. The map's disappearance	28
6. Getting close	35
7. Treasure	46
8. Malkuth	52
9. Search for truth is in the opposite direction	63
10. See that you cannot see	76
11. Now is all there is, yet seek it not	88
12. Jungle life	100
13. The mind knows not itself	107
14. What you value becomes your prison	123
15. Who do you think you are	139
16. The unexpected	151
17. Beware of your benefactor	163
18. Being and doing, the two great powers	176
19. Alicia	190
20. The center of your fear is a great power	200

21. Jungle crisis · 213
22. Being truthful to the moment · · · · · · · · · · · · · · 220
23. Alicia returns · 235
24. Thought is a good servant and a poor master · · · 242
25. Know the two pathways home · · · · · · · · · · · · · · 257
26. Questions and answers · · · · · · · · · · · · · · · · · · · 267
27. A chapter closes · 278
28. The secret of the twelfth Stone · · · · · · · · · · · · · 289

Getting the most out of this book

Most people will read this for pleasure from the adventure perspective. For those who want to practise being present throughout the story, I suggest spending one day on each chapter that relates to each stone, practising the exercises, writing down any insights that affect you personally and start practising the being present exercise from chapter 15, three times every day. At the completion of this book, I suggest reading Breath Integration or Inner Adventures, which cover more in-depth of breath and being present. Then find a Practitioner of Breath Integration or Integrative Presence or Rebirther in your area and go and experience a session with him or her.

Foreword

After thirty years of conducting countless seminars and writing nine books I woke up a little bit to several important insights. The first was that most people do not want to wake up to the magnificence of themselves. How do I know this? Because since I started my own inner journey I battled with my own resistance to waking up to finally discover that resistance is based on fear of the unknown. Waking up takes us into totally unknown realms and this is terrifying for the rational mind.

Waking up requires that how people currently think, feel and behave will drastically change. They may say they want change, but the only change people really want are positive changes; changes in improving their pleasure, power and freedom. No one is really interested in discovering themselves because that could result in loss of the familiar and what they are accustomed too, and the fear of losing their addictions. People simply want relief from their uncertainty, and for someone to fix their longings and disappointments.

Of course, I am generalizing and there are a growing number of courageous men and women who are willing to face the unknown and make the ultimate discovery of themselves. These are the people that this book was written for.

Discovering my own motivations (mostly hidden) and developing a meagre level of self-honesty, a new dawn appeared in my life and the waking up process began. Then the next important insight was in the method of sharing the information and inspiration. Today the human potential movement is oversupplied with a deluge of concepts, systems, techniques, processes, philosophies that all promise enlightenment, or how to feel love, joy and freedom. The market is saturated: some of it is very useful and some not so. How to pass on a totally new and the simple process like the practise of being present in such an over-supplied market was like putting my little piece of straw in a barn that was stacked to the roof with thousands of bales of straw.

Then one day at one of my seminars, a man came up to me and said that the seminar was good, but what he enjoyed the most was being entertained by my stories and antics. I like to throw myself into my work and my first commitment to any seminar that I run is to entertain myself and have fun. I notice that when I am enjoying myself running the seminar, so are most of the others in the room.

So, I took this a step further by looking at the books I'd written, and they were full of intellectual information. So, why not turn my writings also into an entertainment and, with the prompting of Magdalena to write another book on my work of being present, what better way than to dress it in an adventure story?

The secret of the twelve stones – the journey to presence – is based on true events from many of the characters found in the book with name changes to preserve privacy. The setting of the Amazon jungle and the treasure of the 12 stone tablets are fiction, but the inner journey of Harold is real. If you practise being present as described in the book, the inner journey will likewise be yours.

Enjoy and welcome to the greatest adventure of your life.

The Secret of the Twelve Stones

1. Your search for truth will take you in the opposite direction.
2. See that you don't see
3. Now is all there is, yet seek it not
4. The mind is not with itself
5. What you value becomes your attachment and your prison
6. Who do you think you are
7. Beware of your benefactor
8. Being and doing, the two great powers lead you home
9. The centre of your fear is a great power
10. Being truthful to the moment
11. Thought is a good servant and a poor master- Know the two pathways home
12. ?

Chapter One
The Stone Map

The small wooden square box fell out of the hole in the wall and made a loud clatter as it hit the wooden floor. It was about twice the size of a loaf of bread, but quite heavy, from the sound it made on landing. Harold paused, poised to make a second strike against the wall with the sledge hammer, and instead knelt to more closely examine his find. It was very old. Much older than the building he was helping to demolish. It was probably many hundreds of years old. He wiped his hand to remove the dust from the lid and there was very fine writing that had been chiseled into the wood, but it was faded from age and mould. There were two small handles at each end, intricately made, and no doubt this had once been a finely-made small wooden chest.

There was no opening and no indication of how to open it. He picked it up and noted that whatever it contained was quite heavy. Holding it to one ear he shook it and listened for any movement inside. There was a clattering sound of some metal object, perhaps a gold bar, he thought. Gathering it under his arm, he strode off towards Harry's office. Harry was his supervisor as well as a lifetime friend. They'd played rugby together in their youth.

"What do you make of this? I was working in the end room and put a hole in the wall and this fell out."

Harry picked up a hammer and chisel and with one swift blow, the lid clattered to the floor, revealing what appeared to be an ancient square flat roofing tile. Harold picked it up out of the chest and placed it on the desk. It had a fine covering of dust from probably many centuries and picking up a paper tissue from his supervisor's desk he wiped a corner of it. They both leaned to see the intricate carving with now faded paint or dye to help highlight the carvings of some foreign language. He wiped until the whole surface was cleaned.

They both stared silently at what appeared to be a map, finely, carefully and artistically carved by a master carver. They were both struck by what was a work of art of sheer beauty. Harold turned it over and they both saw another and even more detailed carving on the other side.

"What is it? My god, it's so beautiful," Harold whispered in reverent awe.

"It must be many hundreds of years old and I must say it is rather magnificent. What are you going to do with it?" Harry asked.

"Well, I was bringing it to you. You're my boss, so I guess it belongs to you."

"You found it, so I would say it's yours," Harry shot back.

"What if it's a treasure map? It could be worth millions."

"I don't think so. But it looks like an archaeological find for sure and in that way, it could be valuable, and if so, I'm sure you will remember your old friend. No, you take it; I have no interest in that sort of thing. You found it, it's yours."

Harold picked up the stone slab, placed it back in the box and tying the lid back on with a piece of cord lying on Harry's desk, started to leave. Harry called out to him, saying with a smile, "It's probably one of those treasures that are cursed, and you will probably die from some agonizing and horrible plague for finding it. Isn't that how the story lines go?" Harold smiled back.

Before finding this strange object, Harold had reached a crossroad in his life, another one of many. As a young man his search for his masculinity had caused him to volunteer as a combat soldier in Vietnam during the war and as terrible as that experience was, it started his search for truth. Finding himself in the middle of the Communist Tet offensive in 1968 marked a major turning point in his life. Even though the experience left him mentally and emotionally scarred, he had the insight that something wonderful existed beyond normal thinking. After that he drifted from job to job and from relationship to relationship. A brief period in business, and, disillusioned, he was attracted to psychology and then into the human potential movement. Here he found solitude from the pains of the past in yoga and meditation and other useful techniques. It was here that he met his third wife, Helen, with whom he had two children, Marlene and Jonathan. His previous two wives had given him stability and opportunities to grow, but because of his personal issues around his own self esteem, he effectively sabotaged two wonderful unions. With Helen, and through her encouragement, he had found his self-worth. After twenty years of a happy life together, she was suddenly killed in a tragic motor accident. That was six years ago and to hold himself together, he had thrown himself into reading self-improvement books and couldn't get enough of them. Somehow, they took away the pain. He wasn't a wealthy man and with this current find, which appeared to be a map of some kind, perhaps life was smiling on him at last and his financial position might improve. He felt a possible windfall, or a great benefit lay in store for him.

Three months later and Jonathan, Harold's son, was looking at him curiously. "So, what is this all about, Dad? You want me to give up my job and go wading through the South American jungle with you because of some piece of rock that is supposed to be a treasure map?"

Jonathan, in his early twenties, with a glass of wine in his hand, tried to look calm, but his voice gave away some of his interest and excitement.

Harold swallowed a joyful chuckle and, smiling, answered, "You know I found the stone slab with the two maps, one on each side, in that wooden box three months ago while I was still working at Jerry's demolition company. Well, I have had it checked out at the University of Archaeology, and at the museum of South American ancient history. These beautifully carved maps apparently, according to the ancient writings on each side, are supposed to be a description of the site of the greatest treasure in the world that the ancient Aztecs hid from the Spanish 500 years ago. It seems that the Indians were made to give up all their gold to the Spanish, but they hid their most valuable treasure in a place that the invaders would never find, in a place that they called the Valley of the Dead a long way south of their kingdom."

"Go on," Jonathan urged.

"This piece of stone you have been looking at all evening is the actual map to this treasure and it seems that it was hidden in the wall, probably when it was built 150 years ago and I don't know why or by whom. But I found it and what have I got to lose but go and find what is there?"

"Well, I'm intrigued to say the least."

"Come and look at this, Jonathan. See on one side of the stone slab seems to be a wider view of the map and on the other a more detailed description of the local area. The guy at the museum, Bill Robertson was his name, was so helpful and spent nearly a week on it researching both sides and comparing them to modern day maps. He got as excited about it as I was, and I couldn't have deciphered the maps without him. I promised him at least one gold bar when we got back. He was able to isolate the area to the middle of the Jaú National park in Northern Brazil."

"Is it supposed to be the El Dorado treasure that treasure hunters have been chasing for a hundred years?"

"I don't think so, and Bill explored that possibility but couldn't find a single reference to any other treasure that had been written about previously. That convinced him that it wasn't a hoax and all the map references on the tablets matched exactly those on modern day maps, especially the wider view map. He couldn't of course check out the more detailed map and only we can know that when we get there. But, what is most convincing is that a hoaxer would never have gone to the trouble of finding a master craftsman to have such a work of art carved. Also, Bill was certain that the carving was done well before the Spanish ever arrived in South America, perhaps as far back as a thousand years, maybe more."

"Dad, it's all very romantic and you know that I would support you on any such venture, but the South American jungles that are still left are among the most dangerous on earth. It's not like the jungles of Vietnam where you were fighting all those years ago and besides you are not that young anymore and to go chasing after what could be someone's practical joke that they planted in a wall to catch some crazy guy into making a fool of himself. What have you got to lose, you asked? Just your life, and maybe mine too!"

"You know I would never put your life at risk. I have planned the whole thing in the finest detail, with all the latest safety and camping equipment, satellite communication equipment, enough food for several months and all the health requirements. I even ordered a high-powered automatic weapon for you, just in case of wild animals and who knows, maybe bandits. After all, we are in search of buried treasure."

"And against pirates as well: after all, there are always pirates where there are treasures," Jonathan jokingly interrupted.

Harold briefly frowned at Jonathan's attempted joke that he felt was out of place in a discussion of such importance. Jonathan picked up his disapproval.

"Sorry."

Harold continued. "Anyway, there are firearm restrictions in the park, but I have already hired a guide and he will bring a weapon along just in case."

Harold continued for nearly an hour about all his carefully-planned preparations, travel plans and the expected time it would take. As he finished, he added, "But, I understand, if this is not what you want to do I will do it alone or with the guide."

"I didn't say that I didn't want to do it, Dad, and besides who is going look after you if I wasn't there? I must say, you have prepared it with fine military precision. Even if it does turn out to be a hoax, at least with all this equipment, it will be largely comfortable and a rather exciting camping expedition. I've never been to South America, but I need several weeks to tie up loose ends and quit my job. If you've taken early retirement, then you must be pretty convinced. I'm still skeptical, but one thing I've always admired about you is your sense of adventure. Let's do it, Dad."

Jonathan looked closely at each side of the carved map for the tenth time that evening. There was some magical, invitation that seemed to emanate from it. Some hidden power, some mystical feeling that he couldn't put a thought to seemed to touch him at some unconscious level of his being every time he held and looked at it. He placed it back in the small wooden box and turned to look at his father. They held each other's gaze for a few seconds. They had always been close, except for an eighteen-month period after Helen, his mother and Harold's wife, had died 10 years earlier. As they stood together they both sensed that something would happen that would change both their lives forever. It was not a dread sense, but an exciting invitation into some unknown, undiscovered place inside each of them. In those few seconds, something passed between them, some feelings, thoughts and physical sensations that something wonderful, but tinged with danger would be shared by them both. They took a step towards each other and embraced.

Stepping back and looking at his father, Jonathan uttered, "I must be an idiot, but what have we got to lose?" They both laughed.

A month later all preparations for their departure had been completed and one last family meeting to celebrate their adventure was nearly over.

"There is no fool like an old fool," Harold's housekeeper, Gretel, grumbled to Marlene. "It's clear that it is just someone's practical joke against your father. No one finds maps of buried treasure in this day and age, in walls or anywhere else except in Hollywood movies. He was wise to keep it from leaking to the newspapers. They would have laughed him up one wall and down the next."

"Dad will be okay and besides Jonathan will be with him. They have both been working out in the gym every day and I have never seen Dad looking so good for a 57-year-old. They have hired one of the best guides in Brazil. I'm not worried, or at least not too much," Marlene replied.

"What are we to do but sit around and worry for the next three months?" continued Gretel.

"They have all this latest communication equipment and are going to talk to us every day on a computer program via satellite, similar to Skype. If something goes wrong, we can get help in to them very quickly. Besides, Dad always encouraged all of us to follow our dreams, so maybe we should encourage him to do the same. They will be okay, I'm sure," Marlene said reassuringly, with an inner slight twinge of concern.

———————

Chapter Two
The Adventure Begins

The sun was hot and the temperature humid. All equipment had been unloaded from the motor boat onto the two mules and a small back pack for the three of them. The guide, Arizona, ran a final check with his eyes to ensure all was in balance and well strapped to the mules. Arizona was not his real name, which was unpronounceable by most English-speaking people, but this was the closest and they all agreed this is how he would be addressed. He spoke quite good English with a strong Portuguese and Indian accent but didn't speak much. He was around late-thirties or early forties, small in build, but very muscular, with strong Indian facial features.

The journey to this remote region of the Amazon rain forest had taken them 8 hours from Manaus, the closest and largest city in this region. They had flown from the United States into Manaus and here they had picked up all their equipment, obtained permission for entry into the Jaú National Park, and hired a motor boat to take them up the Rio Jaú to the park entrance. Ahead of them were nearly 80 kilometers of dense and uncharted virgin jungle. Several large rivers stood in their way, which is why Harold had purchased the fold-up rubber raft. There were no bridges in this part of the country.

Jonathan's idea of hiring a helicopter to take them directly to the site was unfortunately not feasible. Apart from the fact that the local authorities did not allow helicopters into the region, the map only roughly showed a broad outline of the location on one side, but with intricate accuracy within a square mile surrounding the actual site, on the reverse side of the tablet. They had to content themselves with travelling and searching for the signs that would lead them directly to the site. Harold had estimated that it would take them anything from 10 to 18 days to cover the distance. Once they found the 'beacon', a strange-looking and prominent rock formation of three rocks on top of each other, they would be close. According to the map the beacon could be seen from three miles away, but only from the ground and not from the air, a further ruling out of the helicopter idea. Both Jonathan and Harold had puzzled over the carved line with an arrow that pointed directly towards the Beacon. This had baffled Bill at the museum also. Perhaps it meant that only from this direction could it be found. But that did not fit as the beacon appeared to be a prominent landmark in the area. Finding this would mean they would have found the entrance to the Valley of the Dead. Then they could look for the more specific features shown on the map, which were close to the beacon, such as the small waterfall with a large rock at the top splitting the river to fall on either side.

There was a strange marking shaped like a broken spear on one side of the rock that pointed to the direction they must follow to the next sign. This sign was the most puzzling part as on the map as it clearly showed a snake raised up in a strike position and 10 steps from it in the direction it pointed was where the treasure was buried. A further clue was that there was a cave with its entrance facing the snake. Well, if the cave could be found, then perhaps in the area was something that looked like a snake that pointed the way. They would have to get there first and find out.

Arizona carried a shotgun over his shoulder attached to a sling and would lead the way, followed by Jonathan, who led on a rope one of the mules. Harold, leading the second mule, followed last. Harold and Jonathan each carried a day's survival food pack, miniature gas stove, light-weight waterproof bedding, change of clothes, compass, local map, small first-aid kit with insect repellent, and a small walkie-talkie in case they got separated.

The Jaú National Park, approximately 100 square miles (2,000,000 ha) roughly the shape of a rugby ball of the 300 km-long Rio Jaú extends to the Carabinani river to its south and to the Unini river and its tributary the Paunini on its north boundary. No indigenous people lived in the park, and the small rural population are mostly descendents of Portuguese who lived mainly along the Unini river. Most were born in the region, and still lived in the traditional style of hunting, fishing, and collecting timber, rubber, nuts, oils, resins and gum. Inland there was just virgin jungle, occasionally visited by foreign researchers and sightseers mainly staying close to the rivers and rarely venturing inland very far.

Because of the devastation to the natural rain forests from unscrupulous foresting throughout Brazil, the Brazilian Government had put aside this huge area of land as a reserve for future generations. This made the park restricted to visitors. Thus, permits and stated reason for visiting needed to be declared. Harold had written that they were archaeologists and researching rock formations in this region.

Arizona led them onto an animal trail that made easier travelling. Jonathan looked back at his father. "A bit like being back in Vietnam, eh, Dad?"

"Maybe son, but we lost that one. We are going to win this one though. I feel good about this. I really do."

"I do too, Dad. Let the great journey begin. Let's go forth and do it!"

The first day was surprisingly easy. The mules were cooperative and easily-managed but required regular hits of sugar cubes and apples to remain happy.

That night, after Jonathan had prepared their first major meal, Harold unpacked the light-weight computer and set up the satellite aerial, with the small solar panel to keep the batteries charged and was overjoyed to speak with Marlene on Skype. Arizona set up the rest of the camp, tents and attended to the mules. He placed his tent respectfully away from the others and generally kept to himself. He even ate alone.

"Shouldn't we tell Arizona about the treasure, Dad? I mean, he may know something about it already and could be more help in finding it."

"Shhhh," Harold cautioned Jonathan. "He may be listening from his tent," Harold whispered. "I think at this stage we will stay with our official intention that we stated to the authorities when obtaining permission to enter the park as archaeologists. We don't know if we can trust him either. The greatest treasure the Aztecs had could be more than tempting for any man. Here we are in the most remote place in his country and if he is unscrupulous, his knowing in advance our intentions could put our lives in danger."

"But he will eventually know, especially when we dig it up. Maybe we should bring him in and maybe give him a small share. What do you think?"

"Let's see first. We have at least one to two weeks of terrain to cover first and let's see how he works out."

"I would have preferred not to have brought him, but I realize he is more effective at negotiating our way through this terrain and that is a great advantage. He also knows much of the area so, that is something I guess. But I don't feel absolutely good about him."

"They said at the tour operators' office that he was one of the best guides in the country and so we must trust that, but I also have a strange feeling about him. We should be careful."

Where the first day of travelling was easy, the second day was equally as hard. They had reached the base of a more rocky and mountainous region and the jungle was thicker. Arizona mostly led following the natural flow of the land and animal trails wherever possible. He was followed by Jonathan, who led the larger of the two mules. Jonathan would from time to time relieve Arizona of the lead position. Harold followed up and left signs by placing brightly-colored ribbons around significant trees for their return trip.

They camped up that night totally exhausted and after eating, all turned in for the night early.

Their tents were an effective protection against insects and especially mosquitoes, which appeared in huge numbers just before dark. Setting up the camp required caution because of the constant danger of poisonous snakes and insects. Harold was no stranger to jungle life, having served in Malaysia at the jungle warfare training school for 12 months before his tour to Vietnam. Jonathan, who had spent many years in Australia's outback, was also no stranger to a local wild-life that presented dangers.

Overall, so far, the journey was going well. What the future held would soon reveal itself.

Chapter Three
Harold's Horror

The next day was as hard as the previous one. There were more animal trails, which tended to follow the lie of the land making travel easier, but the terrain was far from smooth with many small rocky hills and dense thick undergrowth. Harold insisted that they stop and rest for 10 minutes in every hour whether they felt tired or not. He explained that it was an army policy while moving through jungle as it was the best way to keep their strength up. Arizona made no comment and went along with the idea, but Harold couldn't help feeling that the other man had some different ideas about the regular stops.

Jonathan had taken a shine to the two mules and even gave them both names: Henry and Charlie. With each stop he would fuss over them and remove some of the heaviest equipment so they would rest also, and then reload just before moving on. He sought out clumps of tasty grass and hand-fed them. Harold was fascinated by how they responded to Jonathan in a cooperative and friendly manner.

The first five days took them deeper into the heart of Jaú Park and into territory that probably had not been visited by humans for many hundreds of years; perhaps not since the ancient indigenous people who lived in this area many centuries earlier. They saw no signs of anything that resembled humanity, like the used bottles, plastic bags and other forms of pollution that littered the tracks when they first started, and that was refreshing.

Harold had tried to lure Arizona into conversation to get to know more about this reserved man, but he kept a distance from the two European visitors. But, Arizona was very thorough in anything he did and each night the camp was set up with Jonathan's help offering the best protection from the elements, wild animals and insect nests. Harold would meantime set up the communication equipment and speak with Marlene on Skype and pass her the latest news of their travels.

They would stop at the end of each day to give plenty of time to set up tents, cook a good meal and relax with a small brandy afterwards. Harold had brought three bottles, enough for the whole trip, he thought. Jonathan attended to Henry and Charlie, while Arizona would put out some traps for small animals that would get caught during the night and provide a meal for him and Jonathan the following day. Where ever there was a small stream, Arizona would catch several small fish to augment the evening's meal and occasionally Harold would share the fish meal, but mostly stayed with his vegetarian diet. There was a lot of wildlife and on one day Arizona pointed out a spotted jaguar 100 meters away sunning itself on an outcrop of rocks. Being downwind from the creature, it hadn't picked up their scent, which would have made it very interested in Henry and Charlie. They were both restless as they knew of the creature's proximity and Jonathan was able to calm them. Also, there were many monkeys in the area that at times made lots of squawking and howling sounds and the occasional family conflict added lots of squeals. The primates seemed to ignore them as they passed underneath their frolicking in the tree tops. Occasionally Arizona would stop and freeze, putting up a hand for the others to do likewise. After a minute or two a snake would pass on its own directed journey.

Even though Arizona carried a machete, only occasionally did he use it to cut a path through the undergrowth and would even travel an extra 50 meters rather than use it. Jonathan was about to question him on it and then remembered that it was not permitted to cause damage to the flora. There were times when it was unavoidable, but Arizona mostly kept to the park's restrictions.

The rainy season hadn't started yet, which was due in a month's time, but it still rained at least every second or third day. Those days made it humid and sticky and it took them a while to get used to it.

At end of the fifth day, which had been a particularly hard one, Harold was relaxing and digesting his evening meal. The sun was just starting to fade through the overhead trees and he was lying in the light-weight foldout hammock he'd picked up in Los Angles a week earlier. It was an incredible invention that supported itself and his weight on foldout aluminum legs and was not only sturdy but very comfortable. He had bought one for Jonathan also who equally loved it. Arizona was content to sleep on the ground on a thin ground sheet.

"Quick, come and see this, Dad!" Jonathan excitedly called out. "My god, this is amazing, come quickly!"

He quickly bounded towards Jonathan's voice and found him with a long stick in his hand, prodding at something in a bunch of ferns close to Jonathan's tent.

"What is it?" Harold called as he reached Jonathan's side, expecting a large snake, common in this area, but what greeted his eyes was a sight from his worst nightmare. There, crouched in the long grass, was the largest spider he had ever seen in his life. He was particularly afraid of spiders, having had a large tarantula crawl on him during his tour in Vietnam. Jonathan kept poking it gently with the stick to make it move, being totally fascinated with this spectacle. The span of its legs was the size of a dinner plate and it was covered in hair, which made it even more terrifying.

"For god's sake, leave it alone!" Harold shouted to hide his panic as he quickly stepped back.

"I bet my mates back in Aussie would love to see this. I mean, Australia has big buggers, but nothing like this," and Jonathan gently poked it yet again. "I wonder if it's dangerous, but it doesn't want to move much."

Before Harold could voice further protest, Arizona's voice, slightly louder than usual, reached them, "Not a good idea, Jonathan. It's not dangerous to humans as it is a bird-eating spider, but you bothering it like that will cause it to shed a lot of its hair and if that gets on your skin you will be itching crazily for days. Step away from it and leave it in peace."

"What if it decides to crawl into one of the tents during the night? Leaving it here could be a worse idea," Jonathan responded.

"Once it sees there is nothing for it here, it will go. Leave it now and it will not bother you."

By this time, Harold was on the other side of the camp and struggling with his fear of the huge spider. "Coming within a mile of such a creature is far too close for me. Shouldn't we put a cage over it or something, just in case?" Harold heard himself say. Arizona just shook his head and returned to his own tent.

"Well, that was the most amazing thing I have ever seen. My god it was big," Jonathan uttered as he made his way to Harold's side. He seemed to have no fear of it. Harold's whole body shook as a river of fear passed through him. Jonathan saw this and placed his hand gently on his father's arm. "I'm sorry, Dad. I remember you telling me of your spider adventure in Vietnam. Are you okay?"

Harold nodded, but they both knew that he was in extreme shock. Large spiders are frightening for most people, but Harold's reaction was more than just being frightened. His eyes were closed and he was breathing deeply as he felt his feelings, a breathing process he'd learned on a weekend workshop several years earlier in dealing with fear. Seeing his father like this, Jonathan stood beside him, feeling inadequate and unsure what to do.

"Is there anything I can do?" Jonathan whispered. Harold gently shook his head and keeping his eyes tightly closed as if to try and blank out the memory of what he had just seen.

Minutes passed, and Harold remained unmoving as if petrified. He felt numb as a way not to feel the terror that was gripping every part of him. His mind was like a lump of concrete and his body felt cold. "I'm here Dad," Jonathan whispered reassuringly, but still feeling unsure of himself, seeing his father like this. Slowly Harold began to return to normal and finally breathed a huge sigh and opened his eyes.

"I'll make you a cup of tea, yes?" Jonathan asked.

Harold nodded and went to his tent, lay in his hammock, and thought to himself. He had many fears about so many things. Why was the sight of a spider so terrifying? What did that represent for him? He knew he still had issues about the war and suspected there was a mountain of fear and suppressed grief about not allowing himself any feelings after Helen died, and many other things. But somehow the sight of a spider, any spider, seemed more terrifying than anything else he could imagine. What was that all about?

Chapter Four
The River Crossing

The river was wide, wild, and running fast.

"What do you think, shall we cross here?"

"Well, we have checked both up and down river and this does seem the best place. I don't have a good feeling about this, but where else?" Harold answered.

Arizona, having reconnoitered up and down stream for the last two hours, without a further word, picked up the end of the longest rope and tied it around his waist, tying the other end securely around the nearest large tree. Gathering up a second rope, he draped it over his shoulder and around his body and, with the two large sticks he'd prepared as walking and stabilizing sticks, he began wading into the swirling waters. The sticks helped his balance as he slowly made his way across the river. Suddenly his head disappeared from view as he stepped into a hole, then reappeared and found another boulder with one foot as he fought the raging torrent to re-establish his balance. He was upright again and slowly moving. Fifteen minutes later he staggered out of the waters on the other side and, glancing in their direction, shot them a fleeting and untypical grin of triumph. Untying the rope from around him and then tying it to a large tree effectively made a one-strand rope bridge straddling the river. He fixed the other rope to a large stone and then, with a cowboy lassoing action, threw the stone back across to the other side. It took several attempts because of the stone falling short. Arizona would pull it back and throw again. Finally reaching more than three-quarters of the way across, Jonathan waded into the river, picked it up and waded back, tying the end to a bracket on the front of the rubber boat.

Arizona waved for Jonathan to follow with the rubber boat that was full of supplies. Jonathan secured the boat to the rope by a climber's metal carabiner and another rope from himself to the boat in case he lost his balance. The South American slowly began pulling the boat across the river. Harold marveled at Arizona's ingenuity at having the first rope anchored on both sides of the river to prevent the boat from being swept downstream.

All was going well until, with Jonathan holding on to the rear of the boat and half way across, a large log drifting down stream suddenly appeared around the bend in the river, swiftly bearing down upon the rubber raft. Harold, seeing the looming danger, yelled a warning but no one heard above the roar of the raging waters. He ran to the water's edge, frantically waving his arms, and caught Arizona's attention, who then also saw the danger.

Too late: the log slammed into the raft, causing it to flip completely over. Jonathan disappeared from view. Harold's panic was rapidly rising as he saw a disaster unfolding before his eyes and was powerless to do anything. His first impulse was to dive in to try and save is son but knew he would only be swept away.

Still there was no sign of Jonathan, and Harold was now frantic. Arizona, keeping hold of the rope straddling the river, sprinted into the water towards the boat. The rubber raft was now half-submerged with a cascade of water pouring over it like a waterfall where it blocked the river's natural flow. Within seconds he reached it. There was still no sign of Jonathan, who had been swept under the boat as it flipped and was trapped underneath, sandwiched between the equipment and supplies in the boat, and the river's bed, held there by the force of the torrent.

Jonathan, holding his breath and knowing the danger he was in, knew that to panic would be his last action. With all his strength he heaved upward to try and force the stack of supplies and boat away from him, but to no avail. He could not move in any direction, as the raging waters held the boat above him, pinning him to the bottom of the river. How long could he hold out? His lungs were at breaking point: for how much longer? The thought of his mother came to him. He remembered her gently brushing the hair from his forehead in a loving gesture. How he missed her, but now she was with him stroking his head and smiling at him. He looked back at her in amazement. She really was here with him. Memories of her flooded his mind and senses and he smiled back at her. He would reach out to her, but his arms were pinned under a large bag of supplies inside the boat. There was no pain in his lungs anymore and he felt her hand on his cheek and forehead gently caressing him. He called to her and she nodded back with a loving smile.

Suddenly he felt himself being yanked away from her. Something was holding tightly to his leg and strongly pulling him away. He tried to stay with her, but he was being dragged towards the surface. The sun stabbed his eyes as his head emerged from the foaming waters and he began to violently cough and splutter, unable to catch his breath. Arizona had his arm and was pulling him towards the rope, yelling something to him. Finally, he caught it.

"Can you stand up? I can't hold you for much longer!"

Jonathan found his feet and, still coughing, allowed himself to be guided towards the rope until he was able to carry his own weight. Jonathan's body being no longer an anchor for the raft caused it to violently sway back and forth, putting a huge strain on the rope. It snapped with a loud crack, sending the rope end curling through the air like a whip, and the raft went careering downstream. Arizona, holding on to Jonathan and the rope, was able to get them both to the shore. Jonathan rolled on his front, coughing up the water he had breathed in. Arizona thumped him on his back, helping the water come out.

Harold, on the opposite side, sat down and a wave of emotion expressed itself in the flowing of tears down his face at the thought of nearly losing his son. "I am such a fool to have risked his life in this way. We should go home. Fuck the treasure." A vulgarity he rarely used. "It's not worth it."

Three hours later they had re-secured the broken rope and safely got the mules across with no further incidents. Once Jonathan had recovered from his near drowning experience, he and Arizona searched for nearly a mile downstream in the hope of finding their lost equipment, but there was no sign of the boat and they returned with only a few items, but over half of their supplies and equipment was lost.

Father and son sat together beside the river in quiet contemplation of their ordeal. Jonathan broke the silence first, saying, "I tried to thank Arizona for saving my life, but he just rudely walked away in the middle of my speech."

"Receiving praise is not part of his culture, I think. I am so grateful to him also and will certainly cut him in on part of the treasure for what he did today," Harold said.

"I saw Mum. Yes, I saw her with me in the river. She was so real, and she was with me as I was drowning. Maybe I was going crazy, but, Dad, she was touching my face and smiling at me. She really was."

They were silent as the memories of a woman who had touched their lives so deeply swirled through them both. Harold hadn't thought much about her for a while and a tear trickled down the lines in his face. He pulled out a tissue from his pocket and blew his nose and gulped back his feelings. "My god, I miss her," he heard himself say, as if talking to the river he was facing.

"Me too, Dad. She was wearing that white dress with the yellow daisies when we were all last together on that picnic two days before the accident. How I miss her."

After a long silence, Harold asked, "Did we lose much stuff in the boat?"

"Yes. Half our food, one of the hammocks and, I'm sorry to have to tell you, the brandy, all our communication equipment, but not the computer. So, we can't talk to the outside world on Skype, but we can send short messages until the computer battery dies. The solar panels and aerial are gone, but we can rig up a temporary one for short messages. Fortunately, we still have the tents, one hammock, and most of our cooking utensils, and cutlery."

"Well, Henry and Charlie will have less to carry. That will make them happy."

"I know how much you like the hammock, Dad, so you have it and I'll sleep on a pile of leaves under my ground sheet each night. I'll be okay with that."

"Thanks, Jonathan, I'm past sleeping on the ground; did it enough in the army."

After another pause, Harold continued, "This is quite a blow and I'm thinking we should turn back and go home. I really got a fright at the thought of losing you."

"Thanks, but no, Dad, we must go on. We still have some food, all the most important equipment and maybe we can live off the land to supplement our diet. I'm sure Arizona's trapping and fishing skills will keep us supplied and I bet he knows many edible plants. And we still have the map. It was just a small setback. Besides, we've come so far, and we must be over halfway there by now. You were never a quitter and I'm not either. You must have got it from me."

Harold smiled at his son's attempted joke.

Chapter Five
The Map's disappearance

"My god, it was hard today, but we must be getting close. I would say about another day, two days at the most," Harold mused.

It was the tenth day and they had adjusted themselves well to the jungle environment with what food and equipment had survived the river accident.

They sat together in Harold's tent drinking coffee.

Jonathan said, "Don't you think it strange that Arizona hasn't asked us about what we are really doing or looking for? He risked his life at the river and still asked us nothing about our mission. I think that is very strange."

"Umm, yes, it is." Harold responded. "It was clear that he didn't take seriously our stated reason on the official forms for entry into the park, because he said that it is interesting that most foreign sightseers write that. So, he knows that we are not archaeologists. Perhaps he is just doing a job and isn't curious about what we are up to. Anyway, look at this. Here is a local map of the area I picked up in Manaus, and see here, where the river forks, is about the same as on the treasure map. That means we are about one day away."

Jonathan was looking over his shoulder, saying, "And if we take the right-hand fork, that should bring us in sight of the rock formation called the Beacon and then the waterfall that isn't on the modern map. I hope it's still there. If your treasure map is still..."

Harold interrupted him in a whisper, "Not so loud about treasure maps. Arizona might be listening from his tent."

Jonathan continued and, speaking much more quietly, said, "We can't be sure how old your stone treasure map is and if it's many hundreds of years old, the waterfall could have been washed away centuries ago. It's a bit dubious to say the least."

"That is the risk we have to take. If it has I am sure there would be traces of its once having been there."

"But we need that sign of a broken spear to guide us to the snake, whatever that is meant to be, and cave," Jonathan reminded him.

"We could search in each direction until we found it if the worst happens. If the food holds out, and Arizona keeps catching and finding food for us as he did today. That bunch of leaves he found was quite tasty once we added a little salt and spices, and it was filling too."

"Okay, Dad, I might turn in. I'm pretty tired." Picking himself up, as he passed his father he gently rubbed his shoulder. "Goodnight, Dad."

"Goodnight, son, see you in the morning."

As Jonathan made his way to his own tent, he didn't see the shadowy figure crouched down and motionless behind the tree next to Harold's tent.

Harold's sleep was restless with many weird dreams. He would wake up and then slide back again into a strange sleeping pattern. At one stage he woke up with a start, thinking something was wrong and that someone was in the tent with him. He reached for his torch and shone it all around, but everything was in order. He lay back and drifted into another strange dream.

"Wake up Dad! Arizona's disappeared and so have all his belongings. Only his tent and the few things he was carrying for us are left. But he's gone."

Harold opened his eyes and it was still semi-dark. He looked at his watch that showed 05:15. He swung himself out of his hammock and instinctively looked to the canvas bag where he stored the stone map. It wasn't where he had put it the night before.

"My god, Jonathan, the map's missing too!" He frantically moved things, searching for the missing canvas bag that held the stone map. Jonathan burst in with a serious look on his face.

"He must have heard us last night, Dad and crept in and taken it. Are you sure it's gone, have you looked everywhere?" he asked, hoping against hope that his father was mistaken. "Maybe look again. It has to be here."

"No, it's gone. Damn it. After coming all this way and just one or two days out and this happens."

"Wait a minute, Dad," Jonathan said thoughtfully. "We have looked at that piece of stone so many times; I know it off by heart. I could draw it if I have to, and surely you can remember it also?"

Harold sighed in relief at Jonathan's insight. "Yes, you are right. But now we know for sure that Arizona knows our intentions. He knows his own country better than we do, and even if we went after him, he would get there well before us. We should pack up and go back. It's over and you don't know how hard it is to say that. Did he take anything else, like Henry and Charlie?"

"No, but he took his shotgun, so he is armed and probably dangerous. We should have brought a gun along too Dad."

"I never wanted the situation to become dangerous or put our lives in danger. If we went after him, he could be waiting in ambush for us both. No, we have to go back, damn it."

"And let him have the treasure? No way! I'm not turning back, Dad. You're the soldier here and your jungle warfare experience is something I need, but I'll go on alone if you are planning to go back."

"Jonathan don't be a fool. You are no match for him if he has intentions to get that treasure, and he's armed. This would be madness."

They were both silent for a moment as the new situation settled in both their minds.

Jonathan broke the silence first, "I'm not going to let that bastard take what is rightfully ours, and I'll do it alone if I have to."

Harold sat still but it was clear that a battle was being waged inside his head as he weighed up the situation.

"No treasure in the world is worth dying for. Think about it, son."

"Dad, you risked your life in Vietnam and, for right or wrong, you believed in what you were doing back then. I know you have changed your views about war since, but when you were my age, you were willing to die for what you believed in. You also taught me that when the going gets tough, the tough get going. You also always said that we came here on this planet to take risks, and not to always play safe. So, let's go and get what is rightfully yours."

"I was talking about emotional risks, monetary risks, not about risking your life for wealth, and this is what we will be doing if we go after him. Besides, we don't know if this treasure is rightfully mine: it probably belongs to the Brazilian people. Yet, I do have a strange feeling that something is leading me to it and perhaps it is something I need to find – but no, it's crazy to even think about it."

In spite of Harold's reluctance, he recognized his own determination and courage in his son and he felt a sense of pride. "I'm going after him, Dad and I have a machete and a knife as weapons and I'd be really happy if you were with me."

Harold, with a deep sigh of resignation, said, "Okay! I can't let you go on alone, but this is madness. If we go after that treasure, will you agree to do it my way?"

Jonathan nodded, smiling.

"Alright, then, we'll go on, but we will take a different route in case he tries to ambush us."

"Thanks Dad. I bargained that you wouldn't let me go on alone. We've come all this way and it has been the adventure of my life. I know you will take every step to ensure our safety, but this is too exciting to resign from. I wish you'd brought a gun or two. That would have evened things up a bit."

"I was hoping against hope that I wouldn't need these, and I am probably a damn fool for bringing them. But they might be useful if for nothing else but for show. I have something to show you." Harold reached into one of the bags on the floor of his tent, feeling around and down to the bottom, then pulled out a canvas bag. He opened it and pulled out two leather holsters, opened one and took out a .38 Smith and Wesson revolver. "I'm not sure whether I like the idea of us carrying weapons. I picked them up in the black market in Manaus that afternoon you went sightseeing. I was approached by this guy who offered them to me and so as a precautionary measure I bought them. I'm still not sure if this is a good idea, though."

"Wow, Dad, they look great. Can I strap one of them to my waist, I mean, we are going to need some protection if not from wild animals and snakes?"

"Yes, I guess so. I hope I don't live to regret this."

"Come on Dad, we are in a fairly hostile environment. I think we need some protection."

"Okay, I think you are right."

For the next 30 minutes, Harold showed Jonathan how to load, aim and clean the weapon. He smiled at his son's delight at his handling, aiming and sliding the gun in and out of its holster like a small boy.

"We really look the part, now, a Dad?" as he gently slapped the closed holster on his waist.

Next, Harold pulled out the modern map. "I think Arizona will try to cover as much ground as he can, thinking that we don't know the way without the map. So, we will follow our intended route until we hit this river, follow it 'til here," he said, pointing to a fork in the river. "I remember that the treasure map said to follow the right-hand fork. We'll look for any signs of him there and when we are sure he's passed that way, we'll then cut inland and do a loop around here. It will probably take us an extra half or even a full day and he may have already taken off with the treasure by then, but it would be the safest. Besides, if the treasure is as huge as the map suggests, there is no way without help he can possible carry even a fraction of it. If he does realize that we can still remember the map, I am sure Arizona will expect us to travel directly after him and this way I suggest we will outflank him. From this direction we should still find the Beacon and then the waterfall."

They both smiled at each other in mutual trust and with a thrill of adventure. "Okay, Dad. I trust your experience because I would have gone straight after him all the way, and I can see in fact that would probably have been rather stupid. I'll go and pack."

He walked away boyishly patting his new-found friend at his side.

Chapter Six
Getting Close

An hour later, after a quick meal, they were packed and ready to move out. Jonathan led, carrying a machete in one hand and his revolver in the other, loaded and cocked with the safety catch on for quick use.

When Harold suggested he should go first, Jonathan protested, saying that the younger man could see better and was also by this time experienced in moving through jungle terrain, and Harold consented.

"Then, remember to move very slowly with many pauses to listen. Arizona knows this jungle like the back of his hand, so move very carefully," Harold cautioned him in a whisper, "And no talking from here on. We must move silently."

"What if I see him, I can't just shoot him?" Jonathan whispered back.

"Of course not! If you see him, put a shot over his head and hope that he surrenders. Only if he threatens you with his shotgun…" He didn't want to end the sentence.

"I understand. I'll be careful."

"I don't think seeing him is going to be our problem…" Harold didn't want to finish that sentence either.

Harold followed Jonathan about ten meters behind, ready to support Jonathan in any dangerous encounter with Arizona, but far enough behind to keep any noises from the mules from being heard above the normal jungle sounds. He led Henry and Charlie strung behind each other. He had a rope in one hand and the revolver already cocked in the other, ever watchful for any signs of a possible ambush. He knew that Arizona probably was even more experienced than him in jungle movement and that this was more than a dangerous situation. He was plagued with doubts about his failure to convince Jonathan to turn back.

His thoughts drifted to the possible foolishness of bringing weapons at all. People only die in such situations because they carry guns. He remembered a book he'd read years earlier on Quantum physics and the huge influence human consciousness had on the physical world and the environment. Violence attracts violence. He further knew that he would never be able to forgive himself if anything happened to his son.

With that he stopped, un-cocked the revolver and with all his strength threw it far away into the jungle. At that precise moment, Jonathan glanced back in his direction and wasn't sure he could believe what he saw. He rushed back whispering loudly, "What the hell are you doing, Dad?"

Harold sat down. "I'm not going on, son. This is crazy. Weapons attract violence and people die. I could never forgive myself if something happened to you."

"So. this is what it's all about? You don't give a shit about me, you're just worrying about your own ass, your own feelings and how you would feel if something happened to me!" Jonathan angrily spat out.

Harold turned and looked at Jonathan as if for the first time as his words found their mark like a kick to the stomach. "My god, you're right. I have lived my whole life like that, thinking I was loving someone, whereas in fact I was coming from the exact opposite place of fear."

"You can sit there as long as you like. I'm going to find your revolver."

As Jonathan left, Harold examined his feelings about what his son had said. He realized that everyone he'd ever talked to and who shared their worries about the people they cared for, was probably coming from the same place as him: fear. He wondered if in fact if he and these people were really loving someone else or were just caught up in their own fears, and not really, as Jonathan put it, giving a shit about anyone else except themselves and how they would cope if something happened to the other person. This was one of the biggest insights he had ever had into love.

Jonathan returned and sat down beside him and started cleaning the retrieved revolver from the mud it was covered in.

"Well you can go back if you like, but I'm going on," Jonathan announced.

"I've been thinking. My head tells me to go back, but something in my heart tells me to go on. I don't know what that is or means, but I generally listen to my head. But in this case, I will follow something else." After a pause, he continued. "Thanks, son, for what you said to me a few minutes ago. It was probably the most important gift I have ever received in my life. I have much to think about concerning my feelings about love. Perhaps, better said, I have much to feel about my thoughts about love."

Jonathan's tone softened. "I thought you would be so mad at me for what I said that there would be no persuading you to go on. I don't know what I said that changed your mind, but I'm glad I said it."

"Now's not the time to discuss it. Let's go. Give me the gun and I'll carry it in its holster. It might come in handy if just to scare you-know-who."

They reached the fork in just over two hours. There was no sign of Arizona, but on carefully looking round, Harold found a broken leaf on the ground, either because Arizona had been unusually careless as he passed this way, or it was broken off from its branch by a passing animal. Then he saw what appeared to be the very faint imprint of a human shoe near the broken leaf. He wasn't sure, as it also looked like the natural texture of the earth. Looking more closely, Harold was sure that it was the path of their previous guide. Harold signaled to Jonathan with a whispered "psst" sound to catch his attention. Harold had earlier that morning taught Jonathan a series of military hand signals and muffled sounds to communicate with each other rather than talking, which could alert their enemy. Jonathan turned, and Harold pointed to the broken leaf and an unspoken message to be even more alert. Jonathan knowingly nodded and slowly moved on with his weapon held in a ready firing position.

Harold "psst" again and with Jonathan's attention he moved his arm, pointing a new direction for Jonathan to follow. Now the danger of ambush was less as they no longer followed Arizona's suspected path and began their loop around to 'out-flank' their adversary.

Even though Harold was opposed to violence, and aware of the danger they were in with the likelihood of facing what he most opposed, there was an excitement of the hunt stirring in him, which he remembered from the operations in Vietnam. This shocked him, but there was no time to reflect on this at this time. He needed all his observation skills to keep them both safe.

Slowly, one at a time, as the other kept a watchful eye, they crossed the small river that was only knee-deep and then found a track used by animals and this made the way easier. By midday they had covered more ground than they had hoped for earlier that morning. Then the way became rockier and more difficult. Handling Henry and Charlie was also becoming more challenging because of it. The mules had become like pets: both men had formed a strong affection to both animals, and Henry and Charlie returned that affection with cooperation and trust. Then suddenly Henry's front hoof dropped through a hidden narrow hole. There was a loud crack as the bone in its leg broke and Henry released a piecing agonizing bleating. Harold bounded the three steps that separated them and with as much care as possible tried to lift the struggling mule from out of the hole. Its bellows were deafening in Harold's ear as he struggled to free Henry. Henry's plight was causing Charlie to also panic in fear. Jonathan raced back and together they lifted Henry out of the hole and the animal fell heavily to the ground, thrashing around in agonized panic. The two men looked at each other, not knowing what to do. It was clear that Henry would not survive out here in the jungle in this condition for very long. Harold looked mournfully at his devoted friend thrashing about on the ground. Henry, wide-eyed, looked back at him in painful confusion. Harold looked around, picked up a large rock slightly larger than his fist, affectionately patted his friend's neck and stroked the side of his snout. He took a deep breath, then struck the rock as hard as he could to the side of Henry's head; the stunned animal lay still with an occasional kick of its leg. He took out his knife and made a deep cut in the side of its neck, releasing Henry from this life. Jonathan watched in horror but knew there was no other way and that his father was acting from love and not violence.

Harold quietly pointed for Jonathan to take up a sentry position ten meters up the track to keep watch, while he moved to Charlie to comfort the stricken mule. Then he started unpacking the equipment from Henry and reloaded it on Charlie who now stood quietly, having been reassured. By this time the corpse was covered with large ants. They were sure that if Arizona was within half a mile of them, which was likely, from the noise that Henry had made he would know their position. Both men knew this was a serious blow as well as a loss of a dear friend. As Jonathan watched for any unwelcome visitors, he contemplated what had just happened and wondered if he was able to act so decisively in such a desperate moment. He was further glad that it wasn't him who had had to do what just happened. He felt a further confidence in the leadership of his father.

As Harold finished reloading the equipment, he felt to look up as if to check the landscape and a smile spread over his face. Forgetting protocol in his excitement, he whispered to Jonathan, "Jonathan, look."

Hearing his name, Jonathan looked in his direction and then to where Harold was pointing. He couldn't see anything that was obviously exciting his father.

"What is it?" he whispered back.

"Come here where I'm standing," he whispered back, remembering to keep his voice down.

Standing together, Harold pointed: there it was! An outline of a large rock formation with two smaller rocks on top of each other less than fifty meters away was looking down on them. It was completely overgrown with vegetation and vines. They had found the first sign. The secret doubt that Harold had held at the back of his mind that it was just a hoax all these months suddenly dissolved. He whispered to himself, "My god, maybe it really is true. Maybe there really is a treasure after all."

"You betcha, Dad! We've found the Valley of the Dead and the treasure is just down there waiting for us."

"My god, son, I've been plagued by doubts about it all this time and this is the first real sign that that map wasn't a hoax after all."

They both looked closely at the modern map to see where the closest river was to where they were standing.

"Look, it's there," Jonathan quietly whispered, failing to hide his excitement. Looking at his compass, he said, "That means in that direction: it has to be."

Off they set and ten minutes later found a small stream.

"Which way, Dad?"

"I don't know, but I'm guessing it's a short way down stream. Let's go that way."

They hadn't travelled more than twenty minutes, when they came around a large tree and there it was: a small waterfall, and in the middle of the river a huge boulder with a strange marking on it. Yes, on closer inspection, it resembled a broken spear and the spear tip pointed to the left of the river. There were no signs of Arizona or any other human at all. A green moss hung from the trees and covered the ground and not even the most experienced bushman could have possibly hidden his footprints. Feeling confident that Arizona was not nearby, excitedly they went on, knowing that they were close to their goal. They walked on looking for a snake symbol, but an hour later no such sign had appeared. They walked back to the river and again tried to follow the spear's point in a slightly different direction and thirty minutes later, still nothing. They returned to the river and tried again in yet another slightly different direction and, nothing. By now it was getting late in the afternoon.

"Okay, let's move another thirty minutes upstream and camp up there for the night and we will try again in the morning."

"It has to be here somewhere. I remember it well on the treasure map, that the snake symbol was right beside the waterfall. That would make it, maybe 100 meters or 250 meters at the most, so why can't we find anything that resembles a snake?" Jonathan complained.

"We'll find it in the morning, I'm sure. I wonder where Arizona is? If he'd followed the left fork in the river, that would eventually take him towards the Beacon, but he would never have seen it because it was completely covered. So, I wonder what he would do then? Perhaps try to pick up our trail and eventually track us to here. We must find that treasure tomorrow and get away as quickly as possible. He's pretty good in the bush and he will eventually find us, so we have only about a day's grace."

That night, as they were preparing to sleep, Jonathan whispered to Harold, "That must have been terrible, to hit Henry and then cut his throat. I know there was no other way, but I'm unsure if I could have done it."

Harold just stared into his coffee mug and made no comment, nor showed any signs of hearing Jonathan. Jonathan knew instinctively that his father was not ignoring him but was in contemplation of the day's event.

"I really saw the warrior in you come out. I'm sure glad I wasn't a Communist Viet Cong meeting up with you and your crew in Vietnam, Dad."

"I don't live in that world any more, Jonathan. Keeping us alive is my main concern right now."

"And finding the treasure, Dad. Anyway, if we catch up with Arizona," Jonathan said, patting his revolver, "he'll have a real problem."

"I hope not. I hope we never see him again."

Jonathan, sensing a painful place for his father, changed the subject. "You know Dad, I've been thinking. If Arizona hadn't taken off with the stone map and if we hadn't followed the path that we did and if Henry hadn't fallen into the hole in that exact place, we would not have found the Beacon."

Harold looked directly at Jonathan, his look saying 'go on.'

"When we left that place and I climbed that tree half an hour later, the Beacon could not be seen from any other direction. I have only just realized that. The Beacon was completely covered with undergrowth and large trees in every direction, except from a fraction of the south side, the exact path we took. Any other approach and we would have missed it. What a stroke of luck! I can hardly believe it. Without that series of events, those three things happening, we would have traveled for weeks and found nothing. We had to approach the Beacon only from that exact direction. That is the most extraordinary piece of luck I have ever experienced in my whole life."

Harold looked back into his mug. "Good lord, you are absolutely right. Now we know what that carved line with the arrow pointing to the Beacon on the map meant: that only from that direction could it be seen. And remember, when we reached that hill 20 minutes later we could no longer see the Beacon. Only from the direction we came in. In fact, if I hadn't looked up at that moment as I sat beside Henry, we would have missed it as well. Because from a distance it was completely covered and only from that exact spot where Henry died could we have seen it. You couldn't even see it from where you were sitting ten meters away from me." He shook his head in wonderment. "That truly is a miracle."

"That means Arizona must have totally missed it and is probably five miles downstream and completely frustrated and confused as to where the Beacon is. What a laugh!" Jonathan chuckled.

"I don't think he is a man to give up. I think we will see him again. Tomorrow he will probably re-trace his steps and come back to the main river half a mile away. Then, no doubt, he will track us on our loop and eventually get to here."

"How long do you think we have before he shows up?"

"Umm, maybe two days, so we have got to find it tomorrow and get away, or his showing up could be a serious problem. He's not just going to walk in but, knowing him, he will stalk us and he's armed, so we must find it tomorrow or leave empty-handed. It's too risky staying longer."

"Well, if we can't find it, I'm pretty sure he won't. So if the worst happens we can head back, leave a landmark and return by helicopter, yes?"

"You and your helicopter idea! Let's see what tomorrow brings before making such plans. See you in the morning, son."

"Shouldn't one of us stay awake, just in case? What do you think?"

"You can if you want, but I feel we are safe from the likes of Arizona, at least for another 24 hours. After that we will need to really be on our guard."

Chapter Seven
Treasure

They were packed, breakfasted and moving out by 6am. They returned to the waterfall with the markings of the broken spear. They realized that in their haste the day before they had gone in a slightly different direction to where the markings actually pointed.

"I can see why we didn't find it yesterday. See, it's due East. Jonathan, you take that direction, which will be slightly to my left. This way we cover more ground. Just be careful of real snakes. We are seeing quite a number around here and some of them are very venomous."

"And we are looking for a snake symbol, right?"

"Yes. Did you tie up Charlie okay?"

Jonathan nodded, and they moved in the direction the spear markings pointed, ensuring that they kept in each other's sight and carefully checking the ground and under every bush for a snake sign. By midday, they returned to the waterfall for the tenth time, exhausted, confused and frustrated.

"I don't know Dad, but there is nothing. What are we doing wrong? We have found every other marking that was described on the treasure map and yet this one is eluding us. What about that tree trunk that looked like a cobra in a strike position, perhaps that was it?"

"I don't think so. I'm sure that tree wasn't here a thousand years ago; but what about that rock we came across early this morning, remember, on our first sweep? The one with the round marking engraved into it? I have a feeling there is something there."

"But, Dad, that looked nothing like a snake."

"We have searched every other possible place within half a mile of this waterfall. Let's go back to that spot."

Ten minutes later they arrived at the rock with a badly carved circle.

"Dad, that's not a snake, for heaven's sake. It was carved a long time ago by some bad craftsman who couldn't even carve a circle. I mean, it looks more like an egg and that has nothing to do with snakes. And, shit, I'm worried in case Arizona's on his way here and we're never going to find this bloody snake." Jonathan could no longer hide his fear and frustration.

"Wait a minute. What other possible symbol could there be for a snake?"

"Well, in Christian mythology a snake represented deceit and evil."

"Yes," Harold cut in. "But in pagan mythology a snake represented being reborn or new growth, because a snake sheds its skin as a way to allow new growth. What could represent something new or being reborn?"

They both said it together, "An egg! Look, what is carved is not a badly carved circle, but it is in the shape of an egg. Shit, we may have found it!"

In their excitement, Jonathan raced back to Charlie to fetch a shovel and pick and was back within minutes.

By this time Harold had paced out the distance and was poking into the side of a bank with his machete.

"Here is the cave entrance and half way between the cave and the rock is where it is supposed to be buried. Here is the exact spot if I can remember the map correctly." Without any hesitation, Jonathan started frantically digging in the spot his father had directed. When he hit a rock, he changed for the pick and then back to the shovel. Harold watched with growing excitement. Could it really be true, after all these months of planning and two weeks of back-breaking walking through the jungle and the numerous adventures along the way, that at last the greatest treasure in all the world, as claimed by the map, was within their grasp? Could he have known when that small box containing the stone slab with the carving of the map fell out of the wall that three months later he would be standing in the middle of the Amazon jungle beside a deepening hole dug by Jonathan, and only minutes away from becoming the richest man in the entire world?

As Jonathan dug, he said between breaths, "I don't understand why they didn't just carve a bloody snake instead of a stupid egg. How the hell were we to discover this treasure if they give us such a complicated riddle for the last marker? It doesn't make sense."

Clunk! Jonathan's pick hit something other than dirt and rock.

Laughing with a joy Jonathan had not experienced for many years, he exclaimed, "I think I have found something! I've got a good feeling about this."

Minutes later the outline of a wooden chest was being uncovered.

"Well, if this is meant to be the greatest treasure in the world, it's only about the size of a traditional pirate's treasure chest like you see in the movies. Even if it was full of diamonds, I don't really think it is big enough to be the greatest treasure. But we are going to find out in the next few seconds." With that he swung the pick down onto an object that was some type of ancient locking system and it fell away. This was the moment they had both dreamed off for so long.

Frantically, he lifted the lid. Inside was a smaller wooden chest. Jonathan tried lifting it out, but it was too heavy on his own. Harold jumped into the hole to help him lift the smaller chest out and onto the ground. They both jumped out and Jonathan placed the tip of the shovel in a gap between the lid and the chest levered the top of the lid off. Inside was an ancient cloth that was in bad condition from age and parts were badly decomposed. Harold was able to make a small hole with his fingers and then, ripping it open, revealed pieces of flat stone slabs like roof paving stones. Feeling down to the bottom showed that was all there was: just stone slabs shaped like roof tiles. Jonathan exploded his frustration to the surrounding trees.

"We have sweated and risked our lives for a bunch of useless bloody rocks! There must be someone laughing their ass off at us right now. What a bastard, after all we have been through for bloody this." Disgustedly he went over to a tree and banged his head against it in complete disbelief.

Harold stood there in shock and echoed the feelings of his son. Never had he felt such a fool in all his life. He could simply not believe that life would hand him such a cruel joke. Harold picked up the top one and curiously looked at the strange markings similar to the map that was carved into the stone slab. It was written in the same strange language as the map. He was about to toss it back with the others when suddenly the carvings began to change before his eyes, and yet they didn't move. A strange warm, almost joyful, sensation came over him and affected every part of his body, and suddenly he found that he could understand the words and he didn't know why. "Jonathan. Come and look at this. Suddenly I can understand what is written here." Jonathan took the stone tablet, looked at it and shook his head. "It's unreadable. I can't understand that."

"Can't you? Well, that is amazing, because I can."

"So, what does it say?" Jonathan asked, his words still dripping with frustration and sarcasm.

"Well, it says, hang on a minute, I have to concentrate. It says, umm, hang on, okay this is what I think it says:

Your search for truth will take you in the opposite direction. Read no other until you understand! Umm, I wonder what that means?"

"It means, Dad that someone is laughing his ass off at our stupidity and to throw salt into the wound has made some stupid sentence that makes no bloody sense to frustrate us further. Shit, I'm going to the river for a swim. And I will call out to Arizona to come and get his bloody stupid treasure. What idiots we are." He disappeared towards the river still grumbling. "I can't believe this, bloody shit, oh hell!"

"**Your search for truth will take you in the opposite direction. Read no other until you understand.**"

Harold rubbed his chin and he was surprised that the great disappointment was transforming into curiosity. "What could that mean?"

He picked up another stone slab. It had the same type of hieroglyphic writings as the first tablet, but no matter how hard he concentrated, he could not understand it. He looked back at the first one. Initially it was unreadable; and then the same warm feeling as before came over him and the words seem to adjust themselves in his consciousness and yet not move physically at all and he could read it with clarity. "This is very strange," he thought, then turned again back to the second tablet, but it remained unreadable.

"I think we have found a great treasure and I don't know why I know that, but I feel we have. I just have to sort out what it all means."

Chapter Eight
Malkuth

They left the so-called treasure site early the next morning and made their way back by a different route. Charlie was well laden down with all the equipment as well as the small chest containing the twelve stone tablets. Both men carried extra weight to spare Charlie from being over-laden. They walked in silence, Jonathan still smarting from the feeling of disappointment of not finding a 'real treasure', Harold feeling curious, a little confused as to what these stones actually meant. The danger of Arizona seemed far behind them. They were passing through an area that contained an abundance of an edible plant they'd discovered. They stopped and both of them collected a sack full that would last them for many days ahead, which Jonathan insisted on carrying. Jonathan had set a trap the night before and had caught a small squirrel-type creature during the night: a trick he'd learned from Arizona. Harold would remain with his vegetarian diet and was content with the sack full of edible leaves.

About midday they came to a larger stream. "I know a trick that I learned in the army: how to throw off a tracker even if they have tracker dogs. We are moving in a northern direction and the stream is running from north-west to south-east. If we walk in the river for the next mile, he will never be able to track us from beyond this point until we emerge. Only then will he be able to pick up the trail again. Which way do you think Arizona would think we would travel?"

"Well, if we are travelling north, I guess he will think we will continue in the same general direction and follow us downstream going north-west."

"That is what I am counting on. The army taught that you travel in the opposite direction to what your enemy would expect, that helps throw your trackers off the trail. Arizona will have to search in both directions, hopefully following the obvious one, north-west, first. That should give us an extra two days on him, enabling us to reach the Parks entrance long before he can catch up with us."

"Ingenious, Dad. So, upstream it is."

For three hours they waded through the waters, leaving no trail behind them except for an occasional hoof mark from Charlie that still looked like a natural shallow hole in the bed of the stream. Harold was rather proud of himself that he'd impressed his son with his special-forces survival knowledge and thirty years after leaving the service was able to put it into practice that could indeed save their lives.

After leaving the river, they changed back to their Northern route and made good time. Late in the afternoon they came across another river and Jonathan looked at Harold, proposing that perhaps they wade in it for a time to really confuse Arizona. Jonathan suggested that this time they go in the opposite direction as before to really confuse their follower. Harold suggested not, as doing this once would give them enough time to get away.

The river was faster-flowing, Jonathan leading and Harold bringing Charlie from behind as usual. Harold normally would follow where Jonathan had placed his feet, but he saw an easier way and stepped onto a rock that was loose. The rock shifted beneath him, trapping his boot against an adjacent rock: down Harold went, having lost his balance. He let go of the lead holding Charlie so as not to drag the mule into the depths with him. His head broke the water surface at the same second as a piecing pain shot through his ankle.

"Oh hell, I think I have broken my bloody ankle!"

Jonathan was quickly into the water and pulled him to the river's edge and up on to the bank. He carefully removed his boot, while Harold lay moaning and cursing this unfortunate turn of events. Jonathan carefully felt around a rapidly-swelling ankle.

"I don't think it's broken, but it is very twisted and badly strained. You are not going to be able to walk on that for probably a week, maybe longer."

"Well, don't hit me on the head with a bloody rock just yet."

Jonathan smiled at his father's black humor and then frowned at the realization of their predicament. He sighed, "Yes, this is really unfortunate. We will need to find a place around here and make a camp in some form of defensive position, in case you-know-who turns up."

"I'm so bloody sorry this has happened. I have put us both in mortal danger, yet again. Oh shit, I hate this."

Jonathan went and fetched Charlie who had remained faithfully in the middle of the stream where Harold had left him. Then he searched for a possible camp site that would offer them some degree of safety and a clear vision of the river, ensuring they would see anyone approaching from the direction most likely a pursuer would come from.

Setting up the tents and securing the site, Jonathan then cooked a meal. Meantime, Harold made his tent and himself as comfortable as possible, and then tried to send a message to Marlene; but the batteries in the computer had finally run out. They were now totally isolated and this was the worst possible time to have no contact with the outside world. He felt a little relieved that the last message the day before was explaining their communication problem and that everything was okay and that there was nothing to worry about. He knew Marlene would just worry if she knew the truth. He managed to include a map grid reference to their location then. So if the worst happened, a search party would eventually find them, hopefully. The walkie talkies still had battery life in them, but without their solar charging appliance, it would only be a matter of time before they stopped working; so they would only use them in an emergency.

He then turned his mind to the stone tablets. He checked a third one, but it was as unintelligible as the second one he'd looked at. Every time he looked at the first one, initially the words were as strange as the others, but then that same odd warm feeling came over him and somehow his consciousness adjusted itself and even though what he read was not in English, he was able to understand it. He also noticed that whenever a thought about anything else entered his mind the understanding of the words faded, and he could no longer make sense of the writings. It seemed that the only way he could read it was to be fully present with the tablet. He experimented and could see that his understanding of the words came and went as he moved his attention from the tablet on to something else and then back to the tablet again. But it only happened with the first one. The others remained unintelligible to him, no matter how hard he concentrated. Then, after a while, the harder he concentrated on the first stone, the more his understanding was not as sharp. He finally realized that being relaxed but fully attentive to the words on the tablet offered the best understanding of it.

His ankle remained very sore and after dinner, with Jonathan's help, he wrapped it tightly to offer some support. But there was no way he could put even the slightest amount of weight on it. He repeatedly blamed himself yet again for putting their lives in danger.

"One second of not being focused on where I was placing my foot and now a week of possible danger. I'm really sorry for this, Jonathan."

"Dad, there has been such a strange string of events in the last week. I'm beginning to think that, and who knows, maybe this is just another one of those strange happenings that were meant to happen. I'd like to see Arizona again. He saved my life and no matter what intention he now has, in a strange sort of way I actually feel some brotherly affection towards him. I'm sure if he comes and sees what the treasure has turned out to be he will probably laugh it off."

"Yes, like you did, I'm sure," Harold cut in. "I hope in some way our strategy of walking along the river in the opposite direction for those three hours threw him off our trail for enough time to get my ankle working again. We should have walked in the opposite direction for an hour or two on the second river as you suggested, instead of crossing it and damaging my ankle."

"Yeah, that was an amazing trick. Was that one of the things you learnt in Vietnam?"

"No, actually, I learnt it from the eighteen months I spent with the SAS (Special Air Service). This was one of their favorite tricks for escaping pursuing enemy and especially if they had dogs. Anyway, we don't know for sure even if he is on our trail. There were times in the last three days that I felt, and I don't know why I felt this way, that he wasn't even after us. And then I felt he was. Maybe it was just my fears coming and going."

"What if we dumped most of the equipment and you rode on Charlie and we head out tomorrow morning?"

"I thought of that too, but Charlie is not such a big mule as Henry was and wouldn't last the distance with my weight as well as the stone tablets for so long. I know what you are thinking! I'm not leaving those behind. Besides, the way back is pretty rocky. I think we have no choice but to wait it out. From tomorrow one of us must be a sentry and watch over the river from that direction in which I think Arizona will probably come from. We will need to keep all noise like talking and cutting wood right down. And no fires at all, that would give us away more than anything. Maybe there is a chance that he's given up on the idea and gone home."

"How are we going to cook our food?"

"At 4am one of us can light a small fire and cook everything for the day. We will have to be content to eat it cold, but at least it will be cooked. No one will be searching for us at that hour. It's too bad we lost our gas cooker in the river incident when you nearly drowned. That would have cooked with no smoke."

"So, do we need a sentry tonight?"

"No, I think we should be okay, but from tomorrow we will need to be on our guard."

"Okay, Dad, I might turn in."

"See yah son. Sleep well. Tomorrow night you will only get five or six hours' sleep."

The sun peeping into Harold's tent told him it was time to wake up. He glanced at his watch and saw it was only 3.15. That was strange. "Where is that light coming from?" he thought. He maneuvered himself off his hammock, picked up the two walking sticks he had made for himself the previous day, and limped out of the tent opening. He could see a strange haze of light coming from over the hill opposite the river, but it was nothing like any torch or lantern that he'd ever seen. It was more like sunlight, but that was impossible as it was shining from the north. He reached back into his tent and picked up his machete and revolver, just in case, and strapped the gun to his side and slid the machete beneath his belt. He slowly limped towards the light, up the hill and crouched down and tried to see its source from below the trees. He still couldn't make it out. Should he wake Jonathan? But despite this strange appearance, he sensed no danger. Against all his previous army training, he slowly stood up. The light was brighter and seemed to be moving slowly towards him and its brightness made it hard for him to see. Holding up his hand to shade his eyes, he suddenly caught the outlined shape of a man standing about twenty-five yards away from him and in that moment, whoever it was, spoke.

"There is no need for alarm. I come in peace."

The light that appeared to be coming from behind this stranger slowly diminished a little and Harold was able to see the man more clearly. He recollected later that at no time during this meeting did he feel afraid: a very strange occurrence given the situation he and Jonathan were in.

"Who are you and where have you come from?" Harold heard himself say.

"My name is Malkuth. I am here to offer you help. Don't be alarmed."

The brightness of the light, which Harold was unsure if it was coming from behind or from the stranger himself, faded and he was able to now see this Malkuth more clearly. A tall man and well-built with broad shoulders. In the semi-darkness Harold could make out that he was dressed in a white gown similar to how people are dressed in Middle Eastern, Arabic countries. His face seemed kind and gentle with strong features. It was a handsome face, and as the man who called himself Malkuth spoke, Harold felt a strange and gentle feeling from him. It felt almost like love, perhaps like brotherly love, and he felt it rising in his throat. He swallowed as if to relieve himself from it, but he could not remember a time when he felt so at ease when meeting a new person. He felt totally safe. He focused back on the stranger and noticed his English was perfect, with an accent that he could not place.

"I have known about your journey for some time. Would you like to understand the tablets, as I can help you with them?"

"How do you know about the stone tablets and about our journey? I don't understand."

"I cannot tell you at this time where I am from and that doesn't matter, but what matters is your understanding of the tablets. And I have no desire to take them from you or cause you any distress in any way."

"How, how do you know about them, have you met up with Arizona?"

"No, my friend, he is a long way from here. I have known about the tablets for a long time and I am aware of the knowledge that they contain. Would you like my help in understanding them?"

"Yes, but, how, what …"

"I know you have many questions and I am sure you will have your answers in time. My time here is short: let us not waste it on questions that you will eventually discover yourself. I can help you with the tablets but the knowledge they contain will mean that your life will be never the same again. Not only will your mind expand, but also there will be an opening of the heart."

"You understand the stone tablets?"

Nodding, the stranger continued. "Behind me approximately 250 steps is a very large tree. You can't miss it, as it is the only one of that size in the area. At midday, come and visit me and bring the first stone tablet with you. We will talk and eat a little. Come alone. If it makes you more comfortable bring your gun, but I can assure you, you will be quite safe. Until then."

He gently bowed, turned and disappeared into the gloom of the jungle. The light disappeared with him. By now, Harold's eyes had adjusted to the darkness and he slowly limped back to his tent and lay down. He tried to recall this strange meeting, but within seconds fell into the deepest of sleeps.

On opening his eyes, he could hear Jonathan quietly cooking and he could smell the porridge he was cooking over the fire. He glanced at his watch, which said 5.47. He pulled himself up and went out to beside the fire. Jonathan looked at him strangely.

"What's the matter? What are you looking at?" Harold asked.

"I don't know," Jonathan answered. "You look sort of, I don't know, different or something. You look like you had a great night's sleep."

"Jonathan, you are not going to believe this. Or maybe it was just a dream. Yes, yes that's what it must have been, yet it was so real."

"What are you talking about?"

"I think, I mean, I had this amazing dream where some guy walks straight out of the jungle with a bright light which appeared to be emanating from him and speaks perfect English with a strange accent and tells me he knows all about the stone tablets and can help me understand them. He also said that Arizona is a long way away from this spot and he invited me for lunch later today."

Jonathan just looked at him very carefully. "An interesting dream or maybe it really happened."

"I don't know. It seemed so real. But I will check out that part of the forest that he, I mean the guy in the dream told me to go to."

I'll come with you to make sure you don't fall and hurt your ankle anymore."

"No, it's okay, I'll go on my own. I'll be alright. There is nothing to worry about. About midday I'll go and I will be maybe an hour or two. I will tell you all about it when I get back."

"Are you sure?"

"Yeah. I'll be alright. No worries."

Jonathan nodded his understanding. In a strange way he also felt there was nothing amiss. So many strange things had already happened that he found himself feeling safer than he had for a very long time.

"I know you had a dream or something that Arizona is not around, but what do you really think?"

"I don't think he is. In fact, I'm sure of it. Go and catch some fish in the river. It's teeming with them. And as a precaution, keep the gun with you at all times. You know, snakes and other beastly things apart from you know who."

"Okay, Dad, and I might have a swim as well."

Chapter Nine

Your search for truth will take you in the opposite direction

As he slowly made his way to the meeting place with this weird stranger, he had no doubts that he had dreamed it. As expected, Harold found Malkuth sitting in what appeared to be a half-lotus yoga position, that he recognized from his own yoga lessons, with his eyes closed, as if in meditation. As Harold slowly approached, Malkuth, without opening his eyes, gestured to Harold to sit on the carpet opposite him. He was struck by the high quality of the fine and thick Persian carpet that covered much of the area of the clearing in the jungle the size of a very large room He sat down and was amazed that such a thing could have been transported to such a remote part of the country, at least 50 kilometers of constant jungle from the nearest civilized town or village.

He looked for a few seconds at this man who appeared from nowhere with no explanation and with an amazing energy emanating from him. Malkuth's face was handsome with a rugged look of strength and experience, his facial features were strong and yet fine. His complexion was dark with no lines on his face and his age was impossible to tell, possibly passing from thirty-five to fifty-five. He was dressed in what appeared to be a deep green robe that was similar to a monk's robe with a white scarf around his head hiding his hair. He could not remember ever seeing a more handsome man and he guessed he was about six foot high, from his memory of him earlier that morning. Aware that this man might be conscious of him looking, Harold closed his eyes and attempted to meditate as he had been taught years earlier.

Harold's mind drifted to the chain of events that brought him to be sitting on a new carpet in the middle of the Amazon jungle with the most unusual man he had ever met. He found it difficult to meditate and so allowed himself to go off on a chain of associated thoughts. Thinking over all his previous studies; psychology, the fringe areas of the human potential movement, yoga, meditation and workshops on breathing, he'd found them more than helpful. Sometimes though, he found some of the people involved ungrounded and 'flaky,' as he called them, with their hearts in the right place. How he came to end up working as a laborer for Jerry's demolition company for the last year of his working life was more on a whim to do something entirely different and he was persuaded only because Harry, the company's manager, was an old friend and needed some temporary help, which lasted for nearly a year until the finding of the stone map. His mind retraced the steps since that remarkable find of the box falling out of that wall until now. Perhaps fifteen minutes passed and Malkuth spoke.

"Welcome, Harold to my home in the jungle."

Harold opened his eyes to the smile of Malkuth and as if in anticipation of a stream of questions from Harold, Malkuth spoke.

"I have lived in many countries and my origin was from Persia or what is known today as Armenia. I know of the stone slabs, having lived in South America for a long time, and they are known in some long-forgotten esoteric secret societies. The treasure of Eldorado was sometimes confused with these stones, which were regarded by the monks of the Aztecs as more valuable than a very large room filled with gold and diamonds. They buried them to stop them from falling into the hands of Spaniards, whose thirst for plunder was at its height at that time. The monks believed that the new visitors from Europe would destroy them in their disappointment that they were not gold or the treasure they were seeking."

Malkuth paused, looking deeply at Harold and then calmly continued.

"Oh, yes these slabs are very special, perhaps not the stones themselves but the information and wisdom they contain. They are very mystical, which is why you, not knowing the ancient writings, by being fully present with them can gleam an understanding of what is written, but not necessarily the wisdom itself. You have probably discovered this already."

"Yes, and why can I only understand the first one and not the rest?"

"That is because they are in a particular sequence and the wisdom is released in a particular way as a flow of energy and understanding. Not that I compare you with a child, but a good example is that a child must learn to walk before it can run. A student first learns the times table before learning high math. The flow of this energy works in a similar way.

And we could talk for many hours about this and in future times we will continue this and similar discussions but let us discuss the first slab. You brought it with you?"

"Yes."

"Look at it and read what appears in your mind as you look at each mark of the ancient writings."

Harold removed the canvas wrappings and held the tablet up and in front of his face. That same strange feeling came over him and as he focused, the understanding revealed itself in his thoughts as if he was putting them there himself. He spoke his understanding out loud.

"**Your search for truth will take you in the opposite direction.** I have puzzled over this since I first read it and I must confess that it makes no sense to me. Isn't everyone searching for some truth, like God, or enlightenment, happiness, love or whatever?"

Malkuth nodded, acknowledging Harold's confusion, and asked,

"Would you agree that a person seeks for something they feel they do not have?"

Harold nodded in agreement.

"And where do most people look for the truth they seek? Perhaps they look for answers in a philosophy, or a great teacher, or system of learning or knowledge, yes?"

"Where else is there to look?"

"Where else indeed!" Malkuth continued. "Looking for the truth outside of you is perhaps one way to find it, except in that finding is little more than a reflection of what is real. It is like looking at the sun's reflection in dew drops or in the sparkle of the ripples on the surface of a lake and calling it the sun. They are only the sun's reflection. So, where can the truth be really found?"

Harold answered. "I have heard it many times that the truth is in each of us, but how do we access it? What is it and how would I know when I have found it?"

"A good question, Harold. How is it possible that someone who comes from a modern European culture as yourself, with no knowledge in ancient language is able to extract knowledge from markings in a stone that was carved 1500 years ago?"

"Is that really how old they are?" Not getting an answer, Harold continued, "Ah, yes, maybe it was because suddenly the sky opened up and a bolt of enlightenment came and struck such..." His attempt to make a joke was meet with a blank expression and Malkuth's slightly raised hand to stop, yet Harold did not feel he was being corrected.

"Was it because I was present with the tablets that somehow influenced them or the energy they contained?"

"Are you asking me or are you suggesting this?"

Harold sat silent, looking at a pattern of exquisite beauty of the carpet he was sitting on that had caught his eye. Then, feeling Malkuth's gaze on him, he looked back into those amazing eyes.

"I don't know how it works, but from what I have experienced so far with these stones, I would say that being present with them is what did it. And I must confess that I am not finding it easy to be present right now."

A gentle smile came over Malkuth's face, "Yes you are. The second you acknowledged your lack of presence brings you to presence. And, your answer of being present with the stone, Harold, perhaps that was what did it. And notice that it happened inside of you and not because of the stone tablet."

They smiled together. "But surely, the energy in the slab..."

Malkuth, still smiling gently, shook his head as if to stop him in that approach. Harold continued, "Okay, so intellectually knowing about the stones is not necessary, but simply being present is, yes?" Harold asked.

"What do you think?"

"So, the search for truth, no, let me say that again and not in a question form. Don't go searching for truth, just be present with what is before me and, and—my god this is amazing. Don't search for truth, just be present with what is, and truth finds me." Harold paused to let this wisdom permeate throughout his being, before continuing. "Be with the truth of this moment and all else will be added to you, to borrow a phrase from the master Christian."

"Harold, when a person feels happiness, does that person go searching for it? When they feel loved, do they go looking for it, and if they feel free, do they go in search of freedom? And where are those feelings, in another person, situation or event or in us?"

"I don't follow what you mean by the feeling being in us, but of course it is us, so what is significant about that?"

"Let's look at it from another angle. A man comes to you and insults you, how do you feel?'

"Angry."

"Yes, angry and that is a feeling, yes? But what caused that feeling, the man's insult or what you told yourself about the man's words?"

"His insult, of course."

"So, that means that whatever happens outside of you has authority over you?"

"No, um, I'm not sure."

"Remember your psychological studies about the fight/flight syndrome, Harold. An outside event happens like being attacked by a wild animal and what happens?"

"How on earth could you have known what I have studied, oh, that doesn't matter at this moment? Sorry, what was the question again?"

"What causes the fight/flight/freeze response in humans?

"Okay, I'm present again. I got it. The second I register the danger; a message is sent from the brain at 400 kilometers per second that stimulates my glands to release adrenalin into my blood stream that stimulates my muscles to run or fight or to freeze, which is not to feel the pain of being killed."

"So, Harold, was it the attacking animal that causes the adrenalin rush or something else?"

"The attacking animal, of course."

"So, what if the animal is attacking but you don't know it is approaching or have no knowledge of attacking animals because you are too young or unconscious or looking in the other direction, would you still have a release of adrenalin?"

"No, because you wouldn't register the situation as being dangerous."

"Exactly, so let me ask the question again: was it the attacking animal that causes the adrenalin rush or something else, like registering the fact?"

"It would be caused by me registering the fact."

"It is true that everything that happens around us will cause us to interpret it according to our beliefs, past painful experiences that will cause us to register the fact in the way that we do, that will stimulate certain hormones to release emotions of love or of fear."

"That's true." Harold responded. "The environment can at best stimulate my own thought-process to interpret the event positively or negatively and therefore release certain chemicals into my blood stream that either creates love or fear, but the actual cause is completely dependent upon what I tell myself about the event, how I interpret the situation. And what I am telling myself is creating huge tension inside of me, so in fact I am creating my own stress. That is amazing. I never looked at that this way before."

"It is crucial in understanding the practice of being present. So, someone insults you, why do you feel in the way that you do?"

"Because my telling myself that this man is wrong for insulting me, which is in fact, me insulting myself."

Harold laughed out loud and continued, "I think that is so funny. All humanity is convinced that the world is so terrible because it does terrible things to them and all the time they are doing it to themselves. What a laugh!"

"We can look at it from yet another angle. The man insults you. Where does the awareness of the insult happen, in the other man or inside your brain?"

"Inside me."

"Where does the feeling of insult happen, in the other man or inside you?"

"Inside me."

"Where does the tension happen, in the other man or inside of you?"

Harold nodded his understanding.

"So, if there is so much happening inside of us, perhaps that is where our attention should be, yes?"

"Oh yes. Understanding this is so great, but society encourages us to be outside ourselves and to see the outside as our authority. If in pain, take a painkiller. Someone insults you, take revenge or pretend that nothing happened; but we still have the tension inside.

"So, Harold. How do you feel when someone insults you?"

"The fact is that I would still feel bad. I can't deny that."

"That is good that you don't deny such a feeling and we will talk much about that later. But, for now, imagine someone has just insulted you, can you do that?" Harold closed his eyes and nodded.

What are you feeling and what is the thought you are telling yourself?"

"I feel not good and the thought is that this person is wrong for insulting me. And probably because a part of me may belief that part of his insult could be true."

"Yes, Harold. Take some deeper breaths. Who are you without those feelings? Don't answer, just internalize it. Who are you without that thought?"

After a small period, Harold opened his eyes. "I would be free."

"Indeed, you would. But this work is not about getting rid of these thoughts and feelings but seeing how they create illusions in us that outside events are real. Outside events are real up to a certain level, but then our interpretations and judgments take over and then we see the illusion, which is self-generated instead of reality. We will return to this at a later time.

"Let us return to the message of the tablet: what do you understand by that?"

Harold picked up the tablet again, paused as he centered himself in presence, and then read it out loud **"Your search for truth will take you in the opposite direction."** When I am searching for something like truth, I search because I feel I don't have it and my actual searching is putting me into the future and therefore stops me from being present with the here and now. Only in being present in my here and now can I experience truth." Harold was silent as the wisdom entered his consciousness and settled deep inside him. "My god, it is so simple and so amazing."

A feeling of self-empowerment came over him. No one in his life had ever taught him like this. By not teaching him anything but asking certain questions that prompted him to discover the answers himself.

Malkuth tilted his head slightly to one side as if to say, 'well done.' Harold continued.

"All those seminars I've done and all the self-improvement books I've read that suggested that there was something wrong with me and that I needed to change, fix or improve myself were actually taking me in the opposite direction."

"Perhaps not, Harold. Nothing is ever wasted, and every experience teaches us something. Even learning some knowledge that is completely false will eventually have a benefit in a deeper understanding of the truth later on. Every person who is seeking a path of truth does so because they are afraid to trust their own inner guidance and are still looking outside themselves for answers to what to believe in, how to feel and how to behave. How long have you been doing that, Harold?"

"All of my life."

"And remember the huge number of benefits you received along the way. You felt good and inspired many times. Perhaps you still looked outside for answers and many answers came and contained in each one was the seed of your awakening that has eventually brought you to the Amazon jungle to find yourself. Humanity is still at the child state and there is nothing wrong with being immature. Humanity is still enjoying itself as a child and eventually each one will wake up and start to find themselves. Nothing was ever wasted."

"Everyone will wake up?" Harold asked

"Yes, everyone, including those who walk the path of fear and violence; the terrorist, the Mafia, the drug dealer, the thief and those who are abusive and manipulative: all will eventually come home to themselves.

There is no such thing as an evil person, just frightened people, and when a person is afraid they will do anything to survive, which is why we have all done so many crazy things: not because we were bad, but because we were afraid."

"Can I ask you a question about what we have just done here? Was it you asking me these things that prompted me or my intuition to find the answer, or was something else happening?"

"It was something like that. That may not be so important but how do you feel, right now, for that is important."

"I feel confident and great. But who wouldn't in sitting with a master?"

Malkuth's hand came up. "Let us be friends and therefore colleagues and not master or student. Such a relationship is not balanced and therefore the flow of energy can never pass between two people in the space of being present. A student will always feel less and a master more and what is mostly transferred is expectation and obedience. Expectation and obedience are what is passed between child and parent, slave and master, and our work together cannot work from such a space."

"But, surely, you are more experienced in being present, which is what it seems to me that we are discussing here. I feel an immense benevolent power from you that must be born from deep experiences of living in the present."

"You are very wise, Harold. Perhaps I have some experience in being present, but that does not make me more elevated than to anyone else. If there is an elevation then it is only in one's ability to see further like a person can see further standing on the top of a mountain, and the person standing at the base can only see to the extent of his or her vision. Consciousness is no different. The person standing at the base of the mountain simply needs to be present with where he or she is standing and instantly is transformed into standing on the mountain top.

"But enough for today! How is your ankle?"

"Still very tender, but I'll survive."

"You will survive? Perhaps this is another one of your jokes?"

"Oh, yes, it is a common saying where I come from and it means in the long run I will be okay.

Can I ask you another question?" Malkuth nodded. "You said at the beginning of today that you originated from Persia, or what is known today as Armenia. I think they stopped calling it Persia back around 1935. It seemed strange to me that you would put it like that, considering that you don't look old enough to have been born that long ago."

Malkuth answered, smiling, "I have always liked the name, Persia. It is probably one of my attachments."

Changing the subject, Malkuth continued, "Can you visit tomorrow, walking this distance from your camp in your condition?"

Harold nodded.

"Then, at the same time and bring the second stone slab."

Chapter Ten
See That You Cannot See

That night there was a violent thunder storm. Harold's first thought was for Malkuth's fine carpet that must be getting ruined in the heavy deluge of rain. His thoughts travelled to the day's meeting with him and he again wondered about this man. He hadn't seen any tent, dwelling or any cooking or fireplace near where they had sat. He concluded that where Malkuth was sleeping was at another location. There were still so many things he did not understand about him; but one thing he was sure about was that this was an enlightened being despite what he had said. Being in Malkuth's presence seemed to change something in him. Jonathan had commented again how different he looked and even younger when he had returned from the meeting with Malkuth. He had also added that Harold's energy had felt lighter and more compassionate. He smiled as he remembered rushing back to his camp like a child, excited to read the second tablet and to see if he could now understand it. He could, but he was disappointed that it made even less sense than the first one. A tinge of frustration came up in him that he couldn't understand the second tablet and so he let his thoughts run with the water that trickled down the bottom end of his tent where it sagged under the weight of water that had collected, dripping a drop at a time into a plastic bucket he'd placed beneath it.

It was now dark outside and he could hear Charlie moving around nervously in the pen that Jonathan had built to protect him from predators and the more regular downpours which heralded the coming of the wet season. Then he heard the soothing voice of Jonathan as he spoke to Charlie to settle him. Both men were fond of the mule and Charlie was more a family member than a working pet. He remembered a conversation between them a week earlier that Jonathan had started.

"I thought mules were supposed to be stubborn and uncooperative creatures."

"So, did I, but I guess it depends upon how you treat them. He knows he's loved and Henry did as well."

"Yeah, I miss that mule. They were starting to come to me as soon as I said their names."

"Well, they knew they were going to get a sugar cube."

Harold felt happy as he thought of that gentle mule they called Charlie. But his heart went out to Marlene and Jonathan, his children of whom he was immensely proud. Marlene had excelled academically in medicine, and then gave it up and went into natural and alternative healing, which surprised everyone. She was probably the most intelligent and intuitive young woman he'd ever known, qualities rare in any person. Jonathan was not particularly ambitious, and work for him was simply a means to follow his passion in art and was more of a hobby than wanting to make a career out of it. Jonathan made it clear that to do it full time would lose the magic from it. He was always cheerful and a joy to be around. When his mother died, Jonathan suddenly disappeared from Harold's life for over eighteen months and he knew that it was because of something he had said at Helen's funeral. He remembered the circumstances of her death, with her driving alone along that one-way street, to be met by a drunken driver at great speed coming the other way, and she had died instantly. The drunk had survived with a few scratches. How angry Jonathan became at him when he had said at the funeral, that for whatever reason he did not understand, Helen had left their lives, and her leaving was meant to happen so they all needed to deal with their own feelings, rather than blaming a drunken driver who had become a part of their reality. He remembered painfully after his speech, Jonathan walking up to him, red faced with anger, fist clenched, saying "That was total bullshit, Dad. That bastard killed my mother and I hate him for it and I find it hard to believe you'd say that metaphysical crap." For a second, he thought Jonathan was going to hit him, but instead, he turned and walked out of the ceremony and Harold never saw or heard from him again for eighteen months in spite of his repeated attempts to contact him. Then out of the blue, Jonathan had suddenly turned up on his front door late one night during a thunderstorm and very angry. For nearly an hour they had stood in the rain with thunderclaps around them, hurling and screaming anger and blame at each other. Jonathan accused him of how he had failed as a father to always be there for him during his teenage years, and his frustration that he felt he had failed as a son in Harold's eyes because of the unrealistic expectations that his father had placed on him. Harold hurled back at Jonathan's laziness to help around the house, his disrespect, lack of gratitude, his uncaring attitude to get good marks at school and his stupid teenage rebellion. Through it all, the death of Helen came up several times, which deeply wounded them both. On and on they went at each other, until it ran out. Then they fell into each other's arms, sobbing deeply and feeling the pain of deep sorrow and the separation between them. In that instant something changed forever in them both, and from that point, their relationship had never been closer. Harold often reflected to himself that it sometimes takes a real airing of blames, judgments and strong feelings to feel the real feelings of love just beneath the surface.

Suddenly, Harold was snapped back to the present when Jonathan's head appeared in the entrance of his tent.

"Can I come in?"

"Of course, son. How is Charlie? I heard you with him."

"He's fine. I gave him another sugar cube and he's settled."

Sitting in a spare fold-up seat next to Harold's hammock, he continued,

"So, where did you go today? I was tempted to follow you, but I resisted, respecting your wish to go alone. But I must say the way you looked after coming back is similar to how you were early this morning. Then you lost it a bit and you had it again when you returned from your walk. Have you found the fountain of youth in those stone slabs or something?"

"I think I have found something better. You remember when I said I could read the first one but none of the rest, but couldn't understand what it meant? Well, it seems that the meeting with that stranger happened. It wasn't a dream. About a quarter of a mile from here, camped up in that direction, is this most amazing guy who helped me today work out what the first tablet meant."

He continued explaining the first tablet and Jonathan showed signs of being impressed.

"Dad tell me about this guy you call, what's his name, Malkuth or something?"

"Yes, his name is Malkuth and I don't know much about him yet and I think he is an enlightened master." Harold talked for some time about his impression of him. At the end they both wondered how, from nowhere, he had found and knew so much about them and the stone slabs. It was a mystery that Harold assured his son he would eventually discover.

"Why do you think he is an enlightened master?"

"For several reasons. Firstly, he insists that he is not, but with the energy that is emanating from him and to be in his presence is more than amazing. Secondly, it is clear that he understands the stone tablets, but instead of telling me, he asks me key questions and I discovered the power of being present myself."

"Can I meet him?"

"Maybe, I will ask him tomorrow. I have another appointment at midday again. He is going to help me with the second tablet. I understand the words that are written but the meaning totally floors me."

Suddenly an extra-loud thunderclap broke over them and a bright flash of lightning briefly lit up the whole area outside.

"Shit," Jonathan breathed.

A hundred yards away, they suddenly heard a tree trunk crashing to the ground. They both looked at each other.

"I don't think we should sleep until the storm has passed. There could be another lightning strike closer and a falling tree could be dangerous. Grab a coat and umbrella and let's sit outside."

"Yes and grab that last chocolate bar I saw by your bed. It might be nice to have something sweet for a change."

They huddled under umbrellas in a clearing, as the storm raged around them with a constant deluge of rain. Small rivers had appeared in several areas of their camp and threatened to wash away the fire place that Jonathan had built.

"Imagine this, Jonathan. Here we are in the middle of nowhere and there is probably no one within fifty miles of us other than Malkuth and anyone with him."

The next morning revealed some devastation to their camp site. A tree a hundred yards out from their camp had received a lightning strike and was still smoking where the part of the stump had been sheltered from the rain. Jonathan spent the day repairing the damage around the camp, and at midday, Harold limped to his appointment with Malkuth through the mud and the small lakes that had formed in his path. He wondered how much of Malkuth's camp and meeting place was damaged from the heavy rain.

As he rounded the path by the large tree, he was dumbfounded to see that the site was the same as the day before, the carpets in the same place with no water damage from the heavy rain. There were no puddles of water or evidence of any rain whatsoever. Malkuth was nowhere to be seen, so Harold made his way to the carpet and seated himself. The carpet was perfectly dry. It seemed that no rain had fallen here at all. How strange he thought. He closed his eyes and started meditating.

After what seemed about twenty minutes he heard a rustle of someone approaching him and felt that same energy of Malkuth. He remained in mediation and fought the desire to open his eyes and look up. He heard Malkuth sit down, adjust himself and then was also quiet as he himself starting meditating. He could resist no more and half-opened one eye and saw Malkuth dressed similarly to yesterday but with a light-blue gown and green scarf, with his eyes closed. They both remained in that way in another ten minutes, when Malkuth gently spoke, "Good day to you Harold."

Harold smiled and slowly opened his eyes. "Hello."

After some seconds, giving time to Harold to come back more fully from his meditation, he asked, "How is it all going for you?"

Harold answered with a question, "Jonathan is keen to meet you. Can I bring him tomorrow?"

"Perhaps not," Malkuth answered, "As our time together is short, but there will be a time when him and I will connect, but not at this stage. How was the next stone?

Harold sighed, "I thought the first stone slab was confusing enough, but this one seems even more complicated."

"Read it out loud, Harold."

"**See that you cannot see.**" If I can't see, how can I see?"

"Perhaps, Harold the basis of understanding the second stone lies in the first."

"Okay, that's a good clue, thank you. 'Your search for truth will take you in the opposite direction.' People search for truth when they feel they don't have it and the striving reinforces their separation from the present moment, right?"

"Yes, but I think you haven't said the most important thing from the first tablet."

"That the truth is in me and not outside." Seeing Malkuth smiling and nodding, Harold continued. "Then to move my attention to what is happening inside of me especially during a crisis increases my awareness and connects me with my power. Okay, I got that, but where do I go from here?"

"You are trying to use your intellect and the intellect is not a refined enough instrument to fathom the depths of consciousness. That is why knowledge, logic and thought cannot penetrate the purity of now. What does your heart feel when you read the words of the second tablet? Perhaps read it again to yourself but read it from your heart."

"How do I do that with some intellectual information that I don't understand."

"All the more reason to leave your head. The head, the intellect, is not designed to find answers. It is not a problem-solving tool. The intellect is nothing more than a question-posing instrument and if you open your heart, the answer will come.

What can help is to breath a little deeper than normal. Breath if possible with the inhale and exhale connected with no pause in between. This will help you connect with your feelings."

"Ah, that is like the breathing I learnt on a workshop called conscious breathing. I know what you are talking about. Thank you, Malkuth, I will remember that."

Harold was silent as he read the second tablet again to himself. Nothing!

"Go into the heart, Harold. Don't try to find the answer. Trying is always done from the head." Malkuth gently whispered, so quietly that he barely heard it, but heard it he did, took some deeper breaths and suddenly his inspiration and intuition began their rhythm.

Even though his thoughts were present, they were not trying to do anything but simply observe everything that was happening. He began to feel the words. The words were no longer important. Then the meaning itself was no longer important. He felt a sense of ease and a sense of being with the words, then he became the words and the meaning was there. Understanding was there, but none of it mattered. He was simply being present. He closed his eyes and his breathing took on a new rhythm, without his control: a gentle breath with no gaps between the inhalation or exhalation. It was impossible to describe how he felt and descriptions in this moment were not necessary. He quietly slid into a meditation and had no idea how long he sat there...

He slowly opened his eyes and looked at Malkuth, who in that instant opened his eyes and looked back at Harold. They both smiled together a knowing beyond knowing. Then, without warning, a huge emotion of, he was not sure whether it was love or extreme joy, overwhelmed him and deep sobs from the very depths of him expressed themselves. Feelings that had been bottled up in him for probably thirty or forty years released themselves and he sat there and poured out, it seemed, every feeling he had ever denied. When he thought he was done, another wave of strong emotions erupted from that buried place inside of him. Then again, another wave and yet another, until finally he felt he was empty and slid back into a deep meditation full of space and lightness.

He was aware of his new friend placing a cup of tea and a plate of food beside him. He opened his eyes and he was struck by the brightness of the colors surrounding him. The multiple shades of green from the trees and plants of the surroundings were striking. His vision was clearer and he felt more than content. Calmly he reached for the cup and tasted a tea that was tastier than he had ever remembered.

"I have never felt this way before."

"Welcome to being present with yourself. The more present you become the more love, joy and inner freedom you feel. Beautiful isn't it?"

"But what happened?"

"Who cares? It is only a rational mind that is trying to take back its power asking such a question. If you feel like it and when you are ready, what is your understanding of the second tablet?"

As Harold started speaking, it was as if something or someone was speaking through him and yet the understanding that was not there a short time ago, now was.

"See that you cannot see is simply being present when you realize that you are not present. I remember, we touched on this yesterday when you said, the second you acknowledged your lack of presence brings you to presence. You were giving me a clue to the next stone, but I didn't pick it up then. I wasn't ready." He stopped as if his old mind was trying to take over and a brief conflict resulted and then fell away and he continued. "When I realize I am lost in a thought, a feeling, an action or behavior, when these things take me over, or capture me, I simply be present with being taken over, or being captured."

Malkuth sat resting his chin on the fingertips of two pointed hands as if in prayer, and gently nodded with each sentence that Harold spoke; he continued. "It is not about using some technique or special process of becoming enlightened, but just being with the truth of this moment however it is. And how are most of my moments? Captured by my thoughts, my motivations and my beliefs; my feelings that try to make me believe that I am those feelings, which in truth I am not, I am just captured by those feelings; and my actions and I am none of these things. They are my functions and when I see my functions running me, controlling me, I don't try to stop them as they are valuable points for me to see what I am doing, and then I can be fully present with still doing them."

He paused again as the rational mind came in again and questioned this last statement. Another brief conflict, falling away, and he continued.

"**See that I cannot see** is waking up to the fact that right now I am asleep; I cannot see anything beyond my rational conditioning, beliefs or attitudes, and therefore cannot think wisely. I see that I am lost in a feeling that belongs to the past and can feel nothing beyond it and seeing how I am acting from fear. I pay close attention to these things. I become present with them when I realize that I am not present.

After a long silence.

"Anything more to add, Harold?"

"No.., except perhaps this. A person doesn't know they are having a dream or a nightmare until they wake up from it. It's the same with this work. It's not about waking up and becoming enlightened." He paused as a profound thought entered him. "It is about seeing when I am not enlightened and the seeing awakens me. And that is all it means, nothing else."

They both sat silently, for no further words were necessary.

Chapter Eleven
Now is all there is, yet seek it not

The next morning Harold woke feeling irritable and could find no reason for it. He felt disappointed in himself: the amazing inspiration with Malkuth the day before made today somewhat of an anti-climax. Everything annoyed him for no apparent reason. The way Jonathan held his spoon while eating breakfast annoyed him. Jonathan's constant talk about the traps he was setting and catching many small animals to augment his diet annoyed him. He explained it away, that he himself was a vegetarian. Also, the fact that they had been for over three weeks in each other's company without a break was bound to cause people to get on each other's nerves. That there were always pools of water all around from the downpours during the night annoyed him, so it wasn't just Jonathan. The good news was that when he read the third tablet he prided himself that not only did he understand the words but also the meaning. Only the last bit confused him.

Having eaten breakfast, he returned to his tent to write some more notes on the insights he was receiving in his work with Malkuth and looked at the third tablet for the tenth time that morning. He decided to break his mood by openly declaring his triumph to the world that he understood the third tablet with laughter.

"What's so funny?" Jonathan called out.

"I can understand the third tablet. Malkuth will be so impressed."

Jonathan poked his head into Harold's tent. "I don't think Malkuth is interested in being impressed, if you ask me."

"Of course, he'll be impressed." Harold replied, with a return of his irritation that showed in his voice. "Every teacher has a natural pride in their students."

Jonathan left, saying, "Sounds like ego to me."

"Since when have you been a student of the tablets, young man?"

"Oops, sounds like a sensitive spot. I'll go and clean up the dishes," and he left Harold mumbling to himself about young men's arrogance and thinking they know it all.

"Good afternoon Harold." And Malkuth waved for him to be seated in his usual place. "You seem disturbed."

"I thought I disguised it pretty well, but to you, I guess not. Yesterday was probably the most inspirational moment in my whole life. After our meeting I basked in the joy of being alive for the rest of the day. Slept well last night, but since waking up this morning, every little thing is bugging the hell out of me. It seems like after yesterday I regressed back instead of going forward."

"So, you have a goal to go forward?"

"Come on, Malkuth, doesn't everyone?" His irritation coming through in his voice.

"Yes, they do, which is why they probably find it difficult to be present with the truth of what is. Having goals in everyday life is essential to being organized and attending to things that need our attention in the day-to-day business of living. Having dreams about beautiful experiences in the future helps to start creating them in our consciousness. But in terms of our spiritual life, having goals to go forward suggests that perhaps where a person is right now is somehow wrong?" Malkuth tilted his head slightly to one side to support his enquiry.

"Yes, you are right. The first two tablets were clear on this. So, why am I feeling so wretched, after yesterday was what can I call it, such a bloody good day?"

"If you look at most people's lives they mostly appear to be happy, successful and reasonably free. The cracks don't appear at all except in a crisis situation or later in life and only then does the real person emerge. Actually, the real person doesn't emerge either, but a series of learned behaviors of reaction, coming from fear. What does get revealed is the true state of a person's consciousness. Crisis situations don't make the person; they simply reveal what is hidden beneath. Most people don't want to feel real with themselves and so deny or hide the so called bad stuff away, and pretend to be happy, loving and the free person. What people show to the world can be compared with a glass of water. You look into the glass and it looks clear and you can think, that person is really successful. A crisis comes along and it's like someone put a hose into the glass and turned it on. Prior to that no one sees the thin layer of mud or sediment lying at the bottom of the glass, and the sediment represents all the denials, the fears, attachments and beliefs that cause people to be judgmental. Every crisis stirs these up.

"That is what you did yesterday. That was a crisis for you. You stirred the sediment in your glass by being fully present with yourself. The water flowing from the hose eventually causes the sediment to pour from the glass as the glass fills with the clear water of awareness. As we start to become more present with our past obsessions about how life should be and associated fears, they come in conflict with the present, where there are no beliefs, judgments or fears. The pathless path of being present is not an easy path to walk. The paths of beliefs, philosophies, techniques, systems, and knowledge are much more glamorous, stimulating, and exciting. They all eventually lead the person to being present, but they are often the long way home.

And, I can see that you are feeling sensitive today. It is natural to feel a little unsettled after such a major integration that you had, and it can take a little time to be fully integrated into your psyche. Perhaps you need time to be present with that. We can work again tomorrow."

"No, I am ready to work now, but why do you call being present a pathless path?"

"Being truly present with the truth of this moment is a brand-new experience: an experience that has never happened ever before. There is nothing to compare it with and so in the walk of being present there are no signposts or instructions or knowledge on how it is meant to be done, because there is no way to do it. Being present, even though described as a doing thing, is doing nothing but being with ourselves and our surroundings and nothing else. A spiritual path suggests a trail that has been walked along before by previous conscious people and was originally made by a very conscious being. As more people walk the path it is more of a following of someone else's path, and so being present with something brand new is not possible until the person finds inside themselves enough courage and inner guidance to strike out and make their own path. The pathless path of being present is exactly doing that.

Yet to be able to create and walk your own path is to first see how we have been following other people's paths and there is always the possibility of following someone else who is less wise than yourself. We can later learn that the path simply went around in a circle."

"Thank you, I understand. This third stone tablet is much clearer than the first two, except for the last part. I will read it, **now is all there is, yet seek it not.** So, it's clear that nothing exists outside the present moment, that expectations for the future and demands from the past are simply ways of viewing reality and not to get addictively caught up in them, or to be present when we do, yes?"

Harold looked for confirmation of his insight, but Malkuth wasn't so forthright in his support.

"That is one way of looking at it, Harold, but tell me about the second part of the message."

"Okay, so, from what you are saying before, and what the tablet is saying, it is not advisable to have goals in one's spiritual life."

"No, this is not what it is saying at all. It is not possible to attempt to live without spiritual goals. Everyone is seeking for truth, whether they are aware of it or not. Most people's truths are love, joy and freedom and most seek for these things outside themselves and wonder why they often end up feeling disappointed.

But the point here is that we cannot turn off searching with the press of a button, as it is connected to our motivations to live. Yet we can start to be present with our need to search. The searching is not the obstacle, but in not being present with ourselves and our searching, not being present with our motivations is what keeps us running around in circles. Seeing our aiming points and feeling the emotions connected is being present and this presence awakens us. If you read this third tablet with your head, it says not to seek the present moment, but if you read it with your heart, it says to be present with your seeking and the seeking stops by itself. No effort is required through the heart. See how each stone supports the previous and the next, so that your understanding grows to the basic message: 'Be here now with the truth of this moment, however it is'."

"Thank you, Malkuth, that makes a number of things much clearer, and I'm happy to say that I fully understood this stone as I read it, not only the words, but the meaning. I have read some very good books about the present moment, so this tablet was no stranger to me."

"I am happy that you understand it. Could you read it again?"

"**Now is all there is yet seek it not.** You used three magical words that I like very much: love, joy and freedom. Thinking about those words I believe that they are the three greatest values on the planet and everyone is searching for them. Of course, they mostly forget that, and go looking for them in other people, like relationships, big business, entertainment and even in drugs and alcohol, but deep down inside themselves they are unconsciously looking for these three big ones."

"Go on," Malkuth urged.

"But the seeking as we covered in the tablets advise against seeking and you clarified that to be present with our seeking and when we are fully present they find us." Harold sat back on the rug rather proud of himself at his little speech. Jonathan should have been here to see him and then he would have seen how impressed Malkuth was. His thinking was interrupted with another question from Malkuth.

"So, you are saying, being present naturally creates love, joy and freedom? I think that is true, but, Harold, I suspect that you have missed the most important point about being present with what is, however it is."

"What do you mean?" Harold asked, a little of his irritation returning.

"What if you have been summoned by your boss because he was unhappy about some aspects of your work and you are sitting outside his office for thirty minutes waiting for him to become free to see you, what would you be feeling?"

"Pretty worried, which comes from fear, yeah, afraid, I'd feel afraid."

"What if you are sitting in the waiting room of a dentist and you have severe toothache, suspecting he or she will have to extract the tooth, how would you be feeling?"

"Afraid again."

"And I could ask you many such questions and each time you would probably come with the same answer, right?"

Harold nodded his agreement, feeling uncomfortable to where this might be leading.

"Tell me Harold, with all that you have previously learned about the present moment from your books, about love, joy and freedom, what would you do to be present in order to come back to the now in such stressful situations?"

Smiling, with a knowing look on his face, Harold answered, "I would bring myself back into my body and the senses and listen to the wind in the trees, feel the warmth of the sun on my face, smell the roses, imagine tasting my favorite food. I would bring myself into my feelings and allow myself to feel my love while kissing a child or someone emotionally close to me. I would think kind thoughts, knowing that my thoughts create what I feel, and I would be in the here and now with my thoughts."

Malkuth looked back at him for several seconds before replying with no expression on his face, and Harold could not determine if he was satisfied with his answer or not.

"You seem to know all about the present moment, having read some good books about it. Harold, look at the tablet and read it again, but not from your head of already knowing about the present moment, but like yesterday, from your heart. Imagine you know nothing about the present moment, forget all you have learned and read it again, from the feeling center."

Another wave of irritation passed over him as he felt Malkuth was playing with him. It's clear what the present moment is. What is he on about, he thought? Picking up the tablet and trying to adjust himself, but the words did not speak to him in his consciousness at all.

"What are you feeling, Harold?"

"I'm feeling annoyed that you are not understanding me."

"Is the feeling of being annoyed much different from nervousness about seeing your boss or dentist?"

"No, they both come from fear. I can see that my annoyance was coming from an expectation that you approve of me and I am sensing that you may not have been."

"Why are you using words of a past tense?"

"Okay, I'm annoyed now that you are not understanding what I'm saying, damn it."

"So, what can you do? Feel these feelings or think of the wind in the trees, the sun on your skin, the flowers, kissing a child?"

After a long pause, as Malkuth's words found their mark inside him, Harold replied.

"No, thinking positive thoughts will only take me away from what I am really feeling, and I'm pissed off." He closed his eyes and sat still for a moment, realizing that many of his techniques of bringing himself into the present moment were suppressing his real feelings and creating an artificial ideal present moment. That was new for him, and registering that fact shocked him. Malkuth's gentle and loving words reached him.

"Feel what you feel, Harold. This is the truth of **your real** moment. Don't seek the ideal present moment. You won't find it, but it will find you when you are truthful to **your** present moment, which is being pissed off. Be present with being pissed off."

Harold felt his annoyance and it grew into what it really was, an anger buried deep in his past. The anger he felt when Helen died, and he covered it up by justifying the actions of the drunk. Now, realizing how terrified of feeling his anger back then, he used his technique of finding the ideal and not the real present moment, in order not to feel his real feelings. He was shocked to suddenly discover that he was just escaping, rather than being real. Jonathan was more honest than him at the time, he thought. The anger of her dying, kept buried for all these years, came up to his throat and threatened to explode. He tried to control it as well as his composure in front of Malkuth. It kept coming up and getting stronger, and with the help of several words from Malkuth, it threatened to explode out of control. "Breathe a little deeper. Feel that feeling. Go to the center of it and be with that pain."

Harold realized that he was holding his breath to try and control his feelings. He took some breaths and finally, the dam of suppressed angers, fears and deep grief burst with a mighty explosion. "You fucking bastard! You killed Helen, you drunken pig!" Harold screamed at the top of his voice.

All the pain of her dying that he had been too afraid to feel came up accompanied with deep sobs. The deep grief of the day before was nothing compared with what poured out of him now. Wave after wave of suppressed grief and the denial of a life time poured out of him. How lonely he felt for all those years after her passing. He would lie in bed in the morning missing her beside him so terribly, and back then, thought about fucken roses.

Suddenly he heard Malkuth's gentle voice urging him to feel his feelings and to feel the sensations in his body.

Another wave gripped him. He remembered when Marlene had asked him what he was feeling through her tears a day after the funeral, he remained strong, so he could support her and buried what he felt even deeper. How lonely he felt back then. How lonely for Helen's touch he felt now. How unfair it all had been. How unfair it is right now. He yearned to be held as a child like never before. Another wave of sobbing gripped him.

Suddenly he felt a pair of strong arms wrapping themselves around him, which released yet another wave of suppressed grief. He felt Malkuth stroking his hair, and a safety he had never felt since he was a very small child in his mother's arms.

Then finally, it was over, it was all gone and completed. Malkuth gently laid him down and disappeared to make a cup of tea. This time on his own was exactly what he needed. How did Malkuth know? He felt so fragile and yet so peaceful and safe. A wave of love came up as he thought of Helen and then of Marlene and Jonathan and he gently cried as the emotions carried him on a cushion of gentleness. Then came a feeling of love and gratitude for Malkuth and another gentle wave of tears flowed.

Half an hour later, having just finished their tea, Harold looked at probably the most important person to have ever walked into his life and smiled with gratitude, "How can I thank you for what you have given me today?"

"Each person is blessed by a gentle hand or a loving smile at some stage in their lives. There were people there for me a long time ago that enabled me to find the pathless path. And you will one day be there for someone else, I'm sure." "I now partly understand the third tablet, thanks to you."

"No, thanks to you, Harold, you did the work and I think you understand them more than partly. So, until tomorrow, then."

Chapter Twelve
Jungle Life

As each day passed both men were adjusting more and more to the life of the jungle. When Harold wasn't involved with the tablets and writing notes about his work with Malkuth, he would hobble about on his walking sticks looking for safe to eat plants and leaves. The few that Arizona had pointed out to him were helpful and he was discovering more by experimenting. He did this by eating the tiniest fragment of a potentially edible plant and then waiting for several hours for any effects that they might be poisonous. Jonathan was against this idea, worried that his father might experiment with a very poisonous plant where even one drop of its moisture could be fatal. On some occasions his experiments did make him unwell for a few hours, but he kept going and soon had documented six species of edible plants. With the sixth discovery he promised to stop his experiments, claiming that they had enough plants to comfortably live on, much to Jonathan's relief. These steps were necessary, as the food supplies they had brought with them were nearly all gone. Only salt and a few spices were left, and this made many of Harold's vegetarian dishes, according to Jonathan, eatable. Harold also discovered several species of palatable berries by observing which ones the birds and monkeys favored.

Commodities like toothpaste, soap, shampoo and other luxuries were also nearly exhausted and they more than once commented on the loss of half of their equipment at the river accident two weeks earlier. Harold had added to their equipment list twenty extra toothbrushes, which had not been part of the loss. This at least kept their mouths reasonably fresh even without toothpaste.

Fortunately, when they had started out nearly three weeks ago, Harold had equally distributed their most essential supplies, like first aid equipment and the host of drugs against malaria and other tropical diseases, between the three of them. When Arizona disappeared, he had left his share behind because, Harold concluded, Arizona knowing the jungle so well probably knew of more natural drugs all around them than the artificial type from the drug companies.

Meantime Jonathan perfected his trapping and fishing skills with a system of nets he'd improvised from Arizona's unused mosquito net. He had also with much practice been able to spear fish with a swift thrust of a homemade spear. Harold was not impressed when Jonathan insisted he watch him on a successful attempt. Harold walked away saying, "Yuk." Between them, they both supplied a surplus of food.

Jonathan also adopted an interest in the local insects and ant population and had read just before their journey began that there are at least 17,000 species in one square mile of Amazon jungle and began documenting his own records. He commented to Harold that if he spent the next ten lifetimes doing this, he might cover half of the thousands of the different varieties of insect species in just this small piece of the rain forest. Harold couldn't stop being a father with his repeated warnings that many insect species in the Amazon were venomous.

They had positioned the camp a good ten yards above the river, because with each downpour, the river level came up an extra yard and on one occasion an extra two yards. The distance to it made Harold's walks for his daily swim and wash difficult. So Jonathan built a track out of rocks and dirt for a smooth gentle slope down to it. Harold was also grateful to his son who happily did half the cooking and all the washing of clothes and dishes. He had worked out a clever way to clean the dishes after a meal by placing them next to a local ant nest: within minutes the dishes were swarming with them. Fifteen minutes later the ants would disappear, leaving perfectly clean dishes. Jonathan would then rinse them in the river to complete the process. Washing of clothes was done by placing each article under a rock where the current was the strongest and after several hours they were perfectly clean. He remembered to do this downstream from where they collected their drinking water, not knowing this the first time he did it, until Harold gently informed him of military jungle hygiene.

One day, Jonathan decided to dig a deep hole for a toilet, that he called the long drop. After a whole day of digging his way through tree roots and rocks he had managed a hole six foot deep. Then he went to a lot of effort and built a toilet seat and a makeshift roof out of large palm leaves that actually worked at keeping the rain at bay. Later that afternoon, when the daily heavy downpour arrived, the hole filled with water from ground seepage and stayed that way for the rest of their stay. Jonathan jokingly declared that he'd built a well instead, but they had to revert back to their normal procedure of going off to a private place behind a tree.

At night they shared good conversation together. Jonathan openly spoke of his sadness over the breakup with his girlfriend, Jane, three months before leaving with his father on this journey. He was ready to marry her, but something changed in Jane and she suddenly disappeared out of his life. He missed her badly.

Harold talked about the fun times while serving in Vietnam. He purposely stayed away from discussing his combat experiences and Jonathan sensed a deep pain around this and stayed clear of any question that might lead there. "You know what I remember the most from it all, was how bloody boring most of it was. The hours of sentry duty, of trying to stay awake, were so tedious.

I do remember one amusing time on one operation when I was on sentry duty, and two enemy Viet Cong, a guy and a woman came within twenty or thirty meters of our position, totally unaware of our presence, and started a shouting match at each other. It was so dark, and this was before the time of night-vision glasses that the modern armies have today. So, I couldn't see them, and now I'm glad because there would have been a different outcome. But, what was amusing is that it was clearly a lovers' quarrel. I couldn't understand a single word, but I smiled at how they were really getting into each other for about ten minutes. The rest of the platoon were so exhausted from the battles that were taking place each day that none of them were woken by it. I remember thinking at the time that I didn't think the enemy was human enough to be lovers. That was the only way a soldier can operate in such conditions, to see the enemy as non-human. That is why war is so anti-life and I will spend the rest of my life working so that you or no other young men and women have to go off and act so inhumanly."

"That must have been funny to listen to. I bet if they knew they were so close to you guys, that would have freaked them out. You have never spoken about the war before. Your work with Malkuth must be creating some healing in you to be more open about it. Tell me another amusing story, Dad.

"Another time, ah, not so amusing but an interesting experience. We were on a patrol in an area that had just been leveled by an American B52 bomber strike the day before and we came across an ancient temple that had been completely overgrown with vegetation and vines. The bomb blasts had done little damage to the temple, but it had blown much of the covering growth away, and I remember thinking that this is probably an important archaeological find. I wanted to explore it, but our section commander said no and so we continued the patrol. Finding the Beacon reminded me of that."

"You should write a book, Dad on all your adventures."

"I don't think I've got much writing abilities in me! But on a lighter note, what are the ingredients of a good story?"

"I don't know, tell me."

"Religion, sex and mystery, so here's a story involving all three. 'Good god, I'm pregnant. I wonder who did it?'"

They both laughed.

"What about this one, Dad? This guy was visiting this tiny village in India back during the British occupation, when things were pretty primitive, and he got dysentery and was confined to his bed in this mangey hotel, unable to move and dying from dehydration. He saw a young boy going past his window and called out to him, if he would find a well with clean water and bring this glass back full, he would give him $10. The boy returned ten minutes later with the glass full of clean water. He drank it and it tasted so good that he asked him to fetch another for another $10. Ten minutes later the boy returned, but the glass was empty: he said that he couldn't get the water because this big white guy was sitting on the well."

"That's disgusting, Jonathan. How about this one I read recently written by a Bill Watterson? The surest sign that intelligent life exists elsewhere in the Universe is that it has never tried to contact us."

Laughing, Jonathan responded with another, "Here's one, Dad: I had a dream last night that I was eating a giant white marshmallow and woke up this morning and my pillow was missing."

More laughter. Each joke got sillier and more ridiculous than the previous one and made them laugh even more.

"You know Dad, with all our documentation of our research, me with my bugs and you with your rocks, we should document our jokes. So instead of having to spend the time to tell the joke we just give each a serial code. The one you just said would be, let's say, J49. We just say J49 and we know the joke."

Harold picked up on the thread and said, "Okay, what about this one, Q33." The surrounding jungle echoed with their laughter at the nonsense of it all.

"How about this one, Dad?"

"Enough of this highly sophisticated storytelling, I'm going to bed."

"Dad." Suddenly Jonathan became serious. "There is something I have to tell you." He paused as he let the feelings come up in him. "Dad, I really love you."

Harold looked, embarrassingly at his feet and replied, "I love you too, son," and then made a quick exit into his tent. He lay on his hammock thinking. Jonathan could always share his feelings better than he could. He admired him for that and felt slightly sad at his inability to be so open. Perhaps with more work with Malkuth, that might change.

This was becoming a special time for both men together and separately, as they each were finding so many new things within themselves. Life was becoming less serious, more fun, and more natural. Both were finding a contentment that neither had ever known in the civilized world. Thanks to Malkuth's comment earlier in the week of the whereabouts of Arizona, the need to keep guard each night seemed unnecessary and the worry of his suddenly turning up was far from any one's mind.

Chapter Thirteen
The Mind Is Not with Itself

"Good afternoon Harold. How are you feeling?"

"Amazing, thank you. I have a question about being a victim.

I felt embarrassed after yesterday's session. As I thought how I had laid there with all these emotions pouring out of me, didn't that make me a victim?

"What is a victim, Harold?

"I suppose someone who feels victimized by something."

"Did you feel victimised as you processed your emotions?"

"Well, no. I did feel angry as I judged a certain person, but with your prompting to feel and move my presence into my body was so helpful. In that moment I really had no control over it except to try and stop it, but I guess that would have been really suppressing my feelings. Instead I just let it happen and felt totally amazing afterwards."

"That was because you released the fear, as well as the tension trapped in your body and the belief surrounding that fear. It was a full integration.

The difference yesterday between you and a victim, even though you are both judging and blaming, but you were conscious enough to complete the process as you let go and surrendered to the feelings. This happened because you were inside and present with them. A victim remains outside of themselves, focused on the outside situation with the blame and therefore the fear and tension are not released, not integrated and then suppressed.

"Thank you, Malkuth. That makes me feel safer to go more into my feelings."

"How did your contemplation of the fourth tablet go?" "Not well. I understand the words, but again, not the meaning."

"Show me." Malkuth read the tablet, nodded his understanding, and then handed it back to Harold, gently saying, "Would you care to read it?"

"**The Mind is not with itself.** The closest I can get to it is that we are simply not present with our thoughts. But we have already covered that, so I am confused."

"Perhaps to first understand what it means is to see the bigger picture of what it means to be a human. What three functions or important parts of you would best describe you as a human being?"

"My intellect, my body, umm, I guess my emotions."

"What else could be a part of you that makes you a living being?"

"I suppose spirit or soul. My early religious training told me that I have a soul."

"Maybe, but do we experience that part of ourselves or do we know it as a theory or as a collection of knowledge?"

"Well, it's a nice theory," Harold added.

"But there is way to experience the deeper levels of consciousness, that you call soul: by developing the capacity to be regularly present with our three functions, the three areas that you described as being human, intellect, emotions and body. Which of those three do you spend most of the time in, where you mostly live and especially which do you retreat to the most during stressful or threatening situations?"

"I hadn't thought about that before, but I guess it would be my intellect. I tend to lose myself in my thoughts, plans, schemes, day dreams; I guess I spend most of the day in my head."

"From your psychology training, Harold, how many thoughts does the average person have in a day?"

"They say that it is about 50,000 thoughts per day."

"How many can you remember, what you were thinking about yesterday and the day before that?"

"I don't even remember what I was mainly thinking about this morning, except my questions around the fourth tablet, and of the 50,000, I probably remember about four distinct thoughts from yesterday. Other than that, I don't really remember much else."

"Why do you think that you could not remember many more than four thoughts from yesterday?"

"I think I know where you are leading to, Malkuth. Perhaps it was because I was simply not present with them. And the ones I can remember is because I was fully involved, present and totally focused on them."

"Being focused is one thing, but if it is an intellectual focus then it is a narrowing of consciousness, rather than an expansion. The intellect can only focus on one thing at a time, whereas awareness has the ability to expand itself on to many things simultaneously."

"I don't understand. What is the difference between awareness and intellect? I thought they were the same."

"May I suggest that they are very different. Intellect has limited functions, which involves rationality, logic, reason and storing knowledge. To find order and meaning, the intellect forms beliefs and this means that it functions in well-defined borders. When you focus using only your intellect, a lot of power is generated, but confined to a small area. There is not an expansion.

"Awareness involves not only the intellect, but also the emotions and the body. When you are present in all three functions, then an expansion of consciousness happens.

"But let's come back to something that you said, Harold, that was significant, that you are not present with your thoughts."

"That's so true. The lights are on but there is no one at home."

Malkuth smiled at Harold's joke. "What process do you think is happening inside you that prevents you from being present with your thoughts?"

"I guess that I am so lost in my thoughts, it must mean that I am identifying with my thoughts, I think in that moment that I am my thoughts."

"Yes, people are so identified and, as you put it, thinking in that moment, that they are what they are identified with. Yet, it is not only with thoughts, but also with the other two functions. Where do you spend the second most amount of time inside of you?"

"Probably my body. I was an athlete and played rugby in my younger days, so thinking about that, I would say that I have a good relationship with my body."

"And, what kind of relationship do you have with your emotional centre, your feelings, Harold?"

"Probably not so great, as I've tended to avoid negative feelings, especially after a course I did on positive thinking a couple of years ago. But why is this all so important?" "Your emotional centre is probably your weakest link in the chain of consciousness, which means that you rarely go there willingly and only do so when forced, when strong emotions come up that you are faced with. And while you have a weak link you will remain in a state of imbalance. The situation is compounded by the fact that even though we mostly live in one or two centers, we are so identified with them that in fact they use us, and not us using them. We become the servant to something that was designed to serve us. Thus, we become so identified that we cannot be present with them. Does this make any sense to you, Harold?"

Harold nodded and answered, "So, it seems that I have been using my positive thinking to avoid my negative feelings and this has had the effect of closing down my whole emotional centre. But isn't it better to feel positive than negative?"

"Positive and negative are simply people's perceptions and interpretations of an experience. There are no positives or negatives in the present moment. Everything just is! It is our judgments about our experiences that create separation and imbalance between our three functions."

Malkuth picked up a stick and moved to the edge of the carpet and drew a circle in the dirt. Then, starting from the centre of the circle divided it into three equal portions. Next, he wrote the letter 'I' beside one indicating the Intellect, an 'E' beside the second, indicating the emotions and a 'B' beside the third indicating the body.

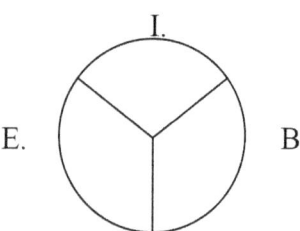

"This is how a balanced person might appear with their three functions, but there are very few people who are that balanced on the planet, which is why there is so much suffering, disproportionate resources and over-population, crime, poverty and war. These are not natural states but the result that most people are living from an imbalanced state within themselves. They are imbalanced not so much because of which centre they spend the most of their time in, but how present they are with each centre."

Malkuth drew a second circle next to the first and then divided it into two equal sizes by drawing a line from the top and down through the centre. He put an I beside one for intellect and a B beside the second one for body. Then drew a line from the centre to the edge of the circle, creating a very small third portion and put the letter E beside it for emotions.

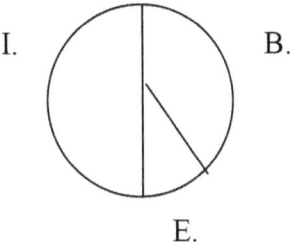

"It is different for each person but this one may look like your consciousness proportions, Harold. Strong intellect, even though you are mostly identified here, but because of the fact you live mostly in it still makes it strong. The second strongest, body and a very weak emotional centre: does that look right to you?"

"No, I would make the emotional centre even smaller."

Malkuth smiled at the self-honesty and Harold's willingness to explore it further. Then he drew two lines from both sides of the circle and joined them at the bottom, which gave the appearance of a tin can looking partly from the top and from the side.

"The circle on the top of the can, which represents the lid, is only the surface potential of what people can experience. This surface is just your three functions as a human and is such a limited and small part of all that we are. This is where most people live and are only aware of their three functions and have no awareness of anything deeper. Yet, because people are rarely present with any of their functions, then they become ruled by the function that they are most identified with and as already said, their functions run them. People don't live through their centers, but these centers live through them and are using them according to their early life conditioning, the way they were brought up in their particular culture, which affects what beliefs they form, the way they emotionally react and how they behave. Does this resonate with you, Harold?"

"Oh yes, indeed. So, this means that this imbalance in the psyche limits consciousness from experiencing the deeper levels, like soul?"

Malkuth nodded and replied, "I don't call it soul because people are so identified with that term, but I refer to it as the true self, but the name is not important."

Harold continued, "Therefore, people live only in the surface consciousness of thought, emotions and body, and mostly in the intellect, and are imbalanced with the other two centers or functions and so, rarely connect with the true part of themselves, yes?" Malkuth, nodding and picking up the stick again, placed in the body of the can three words.

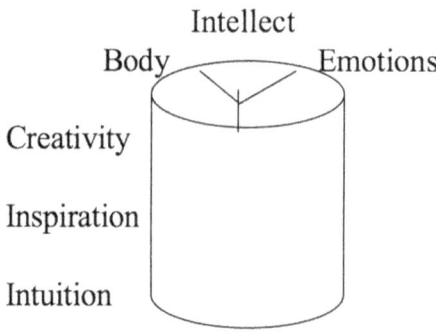

"Creativity, inspiration and intuition: these are not who you really are, but they are closer than the surface functions. Where intellect, emotions and body are the functions of surface consciousness, Creativity, inspiration and intuition are the functions of deeper consciousness or the instruments of the true self. People who know nothing about deeper consciousness would say that creativity comes from the intellect, but I suggest it comes from the deepest part of themselves and often through the intellect, which is why people attribute it as an intellectual function. People say that inspiration comes from the emotions and again, I suggest they come through the emotions and directly from the true self. Most people say that intuition can come from any centre but in fact it only comes through each centre and is a knowing, without knowing why."

Harold responded, "So, what you are saying is there is nothing intellectual, emotional or physical about intuition, which is why science does not regard it as a reality, simply because they cannot define, measure or observe it. Yet, I would say every scientific discovery that was ever made probably was because of creativity, inspiration and especially intuition."

Malkuth nodded and continued. "Creativity, inspiration and intuition are the instruments of our power, and they connect us with the greatest power in the universe. That power cannot be described, as there are no words, no experience that could come close to describing it. Quantum physics has come close to describing a small aspect of this power. Some people have described it as God or the Absolute, all that is, but again, the name is not important, as names can cause a loss of connection through identification."

"How do we train ourselves to access our true self?" Harold asked.

"We can cannot train for it or create it artificially. We are either connected or we are not. We connect with that power by being present. We can however train ourselves into being present by paying attention to our three functions. As our consciousness of each centre grows, the natural balance of the three centers occurs. Not through any technique, belief system or body of knowledge, but through consciousness, by being more aware of what makes us 'tick' as a human. Then we start to live life more from our true nature, which is expressing itself through our three functions."

"This is incredible, Malkuth. So, people are generally not present with themselves and mostly live in their heads like I do, in their memories, day-dreams, imaginings, knowledge, desires and addictions, judgments and intellectual mind games. Oh yes, that's where I live for sure. I remember John Lennon from the Beatles who said many years ago, 'Life is what happens when people are busy doing other things.' What you are saying is that the intellect is only a servant to deeper consciousness, a wonderful servant, but servant nonetheless, yes?"

Malkuth nodded and Harold continued, "So, when the intellect rules, this is what puts us out of balance, and in that state the intellect turns on itself through judgments and creates fear, helped by our past conditioning, beliefs and mental programs of how the world 'should be', rather than how it is. Then it becomes a storage depot for all our fear memories that are held in suppression. Good lord, just about everyone spends 99% of their time living from here. When the intellect is the master, is like letting a seven-year-old child who is bad-tempered and always gets its own way, run the family."

"A good analogy, Harold. The intellect was designed to serve the true master of intuition, but because people have no conscious connection with intuition, the intellect generally rules. When the intellect rules it is very challenging to live in the here and now."

Harold asked, "Can it happen when a person identifies with another center, like the emotions, for example, or even the body and that center will take command instead of the intellect for that person?"

"Yes, you understand it well. An emotional person is totally run by their emotions. The imbalance is increased throughout a person's life by spending more and more time in their favorite center, because of identifying with it almost completely. For example, an intellectual person who has the center of their gravity in the head, is mostly interested in accumulating more knowledge, more beliefs, theories, more systems to stimulate the thinking even more. During stressful times, they would retreat into their rationality and seek a logical solution.

"An emotional person, whose centre of gravity is in their chest, relate to life in terms of how happy they are or how loved they should be. All experiences are first passed through the emotional center and checked for emotional safety.

"A physical person has their center of gravity in their lower solar plexus area and relates to life as to how physically comfortable things are, like the hill being too steep or the rocks too hard or the water being too cold and so on. When stressed they will physically withdraw or strike out.

As you can see everyone has elements of all three but has an unequal quality of presence or connection in each one and this makes being here now quite challenging. This imbalance of living in absence with themselves or living outside themselves makes an excellent point of observation when we see that we are not present with a particular center and this enables us to come back and become more conscious."

Harold asked, "Okay, I understand what being absent means, so what exactly is being present?"

"Being present is not some special kind of thinking, feeling or being, attributed to high levels of consciousness or to highly evolved beings. Being present is simply being fully involved, fully here and now with everything that is happening inside a person and what is happening around them. Most people have little experience in this and so the beginning stage is seeing and feeling when a person notices how they are absent in this moment. Being present is being truthful to the moment, however it looks or is. Stressful situations and life challenges offer probably the best opportunity to come home, but for most people do the exact opposite. They leave themselves even further."

"Could you explain people leaving themselves further in difficult situations a little more?" Harold asked.

"Someone insults you, would you say that is a potentially stressful situation?"

Harold nodded.

"Where is your attention: inside you being aware of your thoughts, emotional reactions and physical tension, or outside on this other person that you are perceiving as a threat?"

"On the outside threat, for sure!"

"Yes, that is how we have been trained to deal with stressful and challenging situations and while our attention, which is the source of our power, is outside of us, we cannot access our own power of creativity, inspiration and intuition when we need it the most: and why? Because we are afraid, and we are run by our three functions instead of us running them. We are outer-directed instead of being inner-directed. We are living outside of ourselves because we have been trained to see all problems and solutions outside. We have been indoctrinated into believing that everything outside is the source of love, joy, freedom and power and that inside there is not much that is worthy enough to examine or explore.

"These stones are the tablets of conscious presence, the ancient art in the practice of being present and awakening. Practice suggests doing something, which in fact is not doing anything except being truthful to whatever enters our field of experience. When we are fully present, living in the present moment, the process of integration happens. Integration means a conscious experience of our completeness – all that we are, beyond creativity, inspiration and intuition. Integration is our natural state, our essential true self, without the surroundings of knowledge, beliefs, techniques or philosophies.

"Science is only interested in two things: the known and the unknown. Being present takes you into a third level, which includes the known, the unknown and the unknowable. The intellect can never penetrate to the unknowable; the unknowable that is beyond consciousness itself. Only by being fully present can you start to connect with all that you are.

"I want to show you a simple exercise that will start your training in being present. It is very simple, and I suggest doing it at least three times every day and the more the better. It only takes a few minutes each time, but it will prepare you to be more present during those times when you most probably challenged, like a crisis situation or when lost in emotions. These are the very times you need to be more conscious and present, but generally most people retreat into their functional center where they feel the safest and lose themselves even further in a function instead of coming to their true self. Are you ready?"

"Most certainly: anything to get out of my head would be more than helpful."

Harold was moved by Malkuth's explanation of the fourth tablet. For all the seminars he'd done and all the books he'd read, this was something new for him. He took a more comfortable position to more readily take in Malkuth's words.

"Close your eyes and take a few deep breaths. Be present with your thoughts. Being present isn't just thinking about your thoughts, but being with each thought, embracing it, being fully involved with the field of energy that surrounds the thought. Catch each thought as it arrives. See that you are not the thought, that these are a function that is happening inside of you. Don't try to control your thoughts. If you have a persistent thought, then be present with that persistent thought. Be with your thoughts and with the energy-feelings they are charged with."

Pausing for about five seconds, he continued. "If you notice that you have drifted away on a chain of associated thoughts, gently return to simply being present with what you are thinking and any feelings around these thoughts."

Malkuth was silent for about ten seconds before speaking again.

"Take a deep breath. Move your attention to your emotions. Be present with the most dominant feeling you have right now. Be fully involved, not looking at your feeling from a distance, but being here now, with and in this feeling. If you feel nothing, then that is a feeling also and be present with the nothingness. If a thought comes, be present with that thought and energy-feeling which this thought has. Push nothing away and be with each thing that enters your field of experience. Be with your whole self, your body and heart with what you feel."

Malkuth was again silent for about fifteen seconds before speaking again.

"Take a deep breath. Move your attention on to your body. Starting from your toes, and in the space of about fifteen seconds slowly move your attention up your body, being present. Be fully involved with the body. Be here now with each part of the body as you arrive at it. If you are distracted by thoughts, feelings or outside noises, pay attention to these things that have captured your mind and then gently return to being present with and feeling the part of the body you were last with."

Malkuth was again silent for about fifteen seconds before speaking again.

"Move through to completion."

After about twenty seconds, giving time to Harold to complete the exercise and to finally open his eyes, Malkuth asked, "How do you feel?"

"Amazing, I feel really present in myself."

"Yes, it is such a simple exercise and it will train you to be more present with your functions and enables you to discover that you are not a function. More importantly it starts to train you in making conscious choices and decisions in the first Point of Power, moving your attention from outside events, situations or outside environment to the inside environment of us where the real part of you begins.

"Practice at least three times before we meet tomorrow."

Chapter Fourteen

What You Value Becomes Your Attachment and Your Prison

Harold woke up with a splitting headache, something he rarely experienced. He lay in his hammock, remembering yesterday's meeting with Malkuth. He recognized the symptoms of resistance in him for the new things he was learning from this amazing man. He was reluctant to practice the being present exercise and couldn't find a reason not to do it, except he just didn't want to. He smiled at himself and his ego, which clearly knew that by Harold being present, it would cease to exist, and no ego wants to give up their power over a person. Harold remembered reading a year ago about the ego. Ego is just a thought form that becomes a mental program, coming from fear with the noble intention of protecting the person from future hurts.

Finding himself sliding into analyzing that increased the pain in his head, he decided to be present with the throbbing in his head instead. Moving his attention directly into the middle of the pain and holding it and being present with it, increased his awareness of emotions he had towards the pain in his head. Holding his attention in the middle of the tension in his head and expanding it to involve his feelings, to his surprise the throbbing stopped, and the pain began to transform into energy. That is remarkable, he thought. The energy was just as intense as the pain, but the word 'pain' carries a connotation of dread and a mental judgment of it being wrong and therefore a desire to escape from it. Where 'pain' described an experience of resistance to escape from, energy was a neutral word that described an experience that simply just was and didn't carry the weight of judgment. Suddenly the headache was just a neutral experience of some energy in his head. This enabled him to be even more present with it and a further surprise happened in that the energy in his head totally disappeared.

He sat up, amazed. 'So, this is what being present is all about.' He thought to himself. 'The point of my attention must be the focus of all my power and when I place it on anything like a tension it restores it back to its natural balance.' He checked in again with the energy that was in his head and yes, it was gone.

Climbing out of his hammock, stretching, he dressed and went and joined Jonathan who was preparing breakfast.

"Good afternoon Harold. How is it all going?"

"Afternoon, Malkuth. Very well, and I made an amazing discovery about being present early this morning. I woke up with this splitting headache and when I was present with it, it disappeared. Is that how it works?"

"Indeed, yes. Whenever we put a tension, a feeling or a disease under the microscope of awareness, the resistance is dissolved. All pain, whether it be physical or emotional is nothing but resistance and identification, and the balance is restored by being present with it."

Harold continued, "After that I spent ten minutes being present with my ankle and I felt immediately something changing or transforming in the middle of where it hurt the most. I feel it is well on the mend. I should be able to walk without my walking sticks in a few days at this rate.

The fifth stone was not very understandable though, but I sense a great importance is hidden in it."

"Each tablet is crucial to the practice of being present. Show it to me."

Malkuth read it, nodded his understanding of it and then handed it to Harold, saying, "Would you care to read it?"

"**Whatyouvaluebecomesyourattachmentandyour prison.** I can understand this with negative things like addictions, drugs and things that we think we need to make us happy. That's clear! But what about love, family, happiness, inner freedom and my new discoveries of being present? I value these things, so how can they become my prison?"

"What is a value and what is a non-value, Harold?"

"Well, I guess a value is something that I believe in and that it is emotionally important to me."

"Yes, I think that sums it up well. So, what is a non-value?"

"Umm, I think it would be something that is not important to me, umm, and something I don't believe in, perhaps a judgment where I am making something wrong, bad or negative when compared with a positive value."

"Yes, possibly so, and is there a difference?"

"Hang on; let me look at the tablet again. Umm, I think I got it. Because what I value becomes an attachment or I form an attachment to it, yes?"

"Are you asking me or suggesting it to me?"

Harold, remembering Malkuth's procedure of never answering questions that he could answer for himself, continued, "I'm suggesting it. What I value becomes my attachment. What I reject in judgment also becomes my attachment. That is because of my desire to get rid of something can cause me to become obsessed with getting rid of it. I understand these words and can understand that negative judgments can become an attachment, but I don't understand how positive and real values like love, joy and freedom can become an attachment."

"So, what is an attachment, Harold?"

"Something that I attach a part of my mind to."

"Like what? Be more specific. Better idea, please read the tablet again from your heart because what you are telling me is not from that place."

Harold picked up the tablet, adjusted himself to it and read, but the words that came back were still coming from his intellect and mixed with past knowledge.

"I think I'm trying too hard. Give me a second to relax and get into my feelings."

Slowly he gradually began to move from his head down into his feelings and the words on the tablet entered his consciousness on that feeling level. Instead of understanding, he began to feel the words that entered his mind. He had experienced this with the first three tablets, but he seemed to go even more deeply with this fourth one. Placing the tablet back beside him, tears brimmed his eyes with the inspiration of what was in his heart, and he spoke with a natural knowing, directly from his intuition instead of his knowledge.

"Life just is. Love just is. It is pure as it is, and nothing need be added to it. It is here now or never."

Malkuth took up his usual posture of his chin resting on the tips of his fingers, as if in prayer, as he listened to the voice that was coming directly from Harold's true self.

"Being present is not a path but is the truth expressing itself. Therefore, being present has no direction, purpose or value, it just is. Being present cannot be measured. The present moment has no value, for value is something that can be measured through comparison. The moment you compare it, the ego has given it a value.

"I leave the present moment when I make a value out of love, by comparing it to when there is no love. My comparing has placed a value on it and that value has become an attachment that is an artificial condition that was not there before, a condition that satisfies a fear in me of not being loved. And so, it becomes my prison because of me need of something not real."

He paused to let the words that came from his lips settle in deeper levels of himself. Then he continued.

"In the present moment, love has no value. Love just is. It is a complete state. It is an end to itself. Therefore, it has no direction, purpose or value. The moment I put a value on it I have compared it, I have added something foreign to it and I have lost its purity. Without comparison there is no value, direction or purpose. Direction is going somewhere because of purpose, and to get there is done in time. Being present, there is no time. There is just now."

He paused again and the wisdom within the words was paving a new pathway from his psyche to his true self. He momentarily reflected that the words that came from his mouth seemed to come from somewhere or from someone else, an inspiration that was happening in him for the first time. He continued.

"That means that in the present moment even life has no purpose. Purpose always means that there is something even more valuable beyond itself; a means to some greater end, to some greater purpose. Life has no purpose, it just is. If life had a purpose it would mean that there was something more valuable than life. If love had a purpose it would mean that there was something more valuable than love. And I can only know these things by leaving the present moment by comparing. It is only our ego and intellect that have been tricking us all this time by making us believe that there is something more valuable beyond itself. We have made religions out of it."

He stopped. A tear of inspiration ran down his cheek and onto his nose and formed a drip on the end. He wiped it away. His understanding of the fourth tablet crystallized in his consciousness and now he spoke more as a reflection.

"Now I understand what Christ was talking about when he said, 'If you want to follow me, give up your family and your possessions and only then can you enter the Kingdom of Heaven.' Heaven being in the here and now and not in some place we go to in the future. I was always confused by these words of giving up family and possessions, thinking that I must literally give up everything, but all he was saying was to keep them, but give up your attachments to them. Give up your addictions to them and only then can a person live in the here and now. He was a true practitioner of being present.

People live in fear of losing their possessions because they have made them valuable. The value is not so much in the person or the possession but in the benefit of what we believe we get from that person or possession. The person or possession is only a means to satisfy our need of them; to satisfy our addiction of them. We have made them valuable because we are not present with them and being present we would see this.

So, the separation from our self is that we have lost ourselves in attachments, so all we have to do is eliminate our attachments and we are free."

Recognizing that Harold had strayed back into his intellect, Malkuth replied, "I think you are missing an important point here, Harold. What is the energy behind wanting to eliminate attachments?"

"Umm, I guess making them wrong, so that must be a judgment."

"Where do judgments come from?"

"Oh yes, I see. My judgments are a result of my comparing, which come from fear. So, it's not about getting rid of attachments, but being fully present with them when they happen. Then they dissolve like my headache did this morning. I'm starting to get it. Then, I can really enjoy my possessions because there is no fear of losing them. In fact, I love people more because there is no threat of loss, no fear of manipulation. Manipulation can only happen because of fear of loss. This is really the secret to a fully-conscious relationship. I enjoy them while they are here, and I enjoy myself when they are not. What incredible but simple wisdom!"

Malkuth spoke. "What you have said, is most eloquent. Please continue."

"I remember reading a story written by Tranxu, the great Chinese sage that highlights this"

Malkuth smiled at Harold's need to climb back into his knowledge for verification and knew that this too will pass as his friend's level of presence expanded."

"When the archer shoots with no prize in mind, he has all his skills; when he shoots to win a brass buckle, he is already nervous; when he shoots for a gold prize, he goes blind, sees two targets, and is out of his mind. His skill has not changed, but the prize divides him. He cares! He thinks more of winning than of shooting, and the need to win drains him of power. Power, meaning presence in our context.

I understand that story now. I guess that's what most people do. They have made going for some goal more important than being present with themselves. When they relax and release their attachments about results, they have all their power, their skills to enjoy the process and achieve it at the same time. Can you add something, Malkuth?"

"It is interesting to note that in society, values are important because they are a means of motivating other people, and can even be a means to control, and as you point out, especially with relationships. Would you agree, Harold that a value is simply a belief that becomes an attachment?"

"Yes, I can see that."

Malkuth continued, "And as you also said so eloquently, a value is something that can be measured by comparison. The intellect appreciates the value of everything, especially qualities that can be measured in people. Attractiveness in people can be measured by good looks, personality, behaviors, fashion and the application of cosmetics because people believe in these things. They are valuable because people trade them for other valuable things like attention, sex, money and even love. Education is valuable because people get knowledge and then they are intellectually valuable. They can get a good job and money.

Society is a system of hierarchy that is based upon how valuable a person is. That is why the hierarchy of society with professors, experts, masters, teachers, gurus, saviors are important. It gives us value. But it is like an empty shell as it adds nothing to our true self and can even be an obstacle to finding ourselves.

Society puts values on everything because it is never present with itself. If it was present in the here and now, it would know that nothing is valuable without attachment, it just is. This is not a judgment on society. It's not wrong, but simply that is the way it is at this stage of its evolution.

Another interesting thing in what you said, Harold, is that in the present moment direction, purpose and value are meaningless. Values, beliefs and philosophies are not wrong, but they can be an obstacle of identification from being present, because the more values a person has, the more opinions, comparisons, judgments, resistances, analyses and identifications they will have; the more attachments they have the more they will be prevented from being present."

Harold jumped in with, "Yes, the pathless path sees that people who need to be valuable is because they have missed the essence of who they really are and who they really are has no description. Their ego demands that they be respected, acknowledged and loved, not only for who they think they are, but for what they can do. People become slaves and addicted to being valuable in order to being loved. So, being valuable means to get others to love them."

"Quite possibly, Harold, as a person practices being present, they could start to see this as one of the great spiritual traps. While a person seeks to be loved from the outside, the inner world is neglected. The true self is not afraid to be useless and to be without value. And when present, the person goes beyond ego to arrive at oneness, and experiences his or her completeness."

Harold followed on, "I can see that values actually separate people and that every conflict in history has been caused by two sides with opposing values. The more values I have, the more I will come into conflict with other opposing values. The more values I have, the more distant I will be from my true self. In the here and now there are no beliefs or values, just a sense of being-ness. The purity of being alone with myself and life with no value, direction or purpose, is trusting my own intuition. I think many intellectual people would find this rather shocking. Wow!"

Harold burst out laughing at the irony of it all and then continued. "So, what is the meaning of life? As was written in the immortal words from the 'Hitchhiker's Guide to the Galaxy', the meaning of life is the number 42."

Malkuth also started laughing, and between chuckles: "What, 42?"

Harold continued between his laughter, "The story goes that they built this computer that could answer every single question in the universe and so they asked it the meaning of life. It was a difficult question and it took the computer 10 million years to find the answer. And the people gathered around and out came the answer, 42. The people were confused so they asked the computer what does 42 mean? Another difficult question, and it took the computer another 10 million years and finally the answer came. The people gathered again, and the answer came: 42 is the meaning of life."

They both again laughed. "Harold, you are a great story teller."

"I'm not entirely sure if that was how the original story from the book was, but I find it not only amusing, but quite accurate in people's meaningless search to find meaning."

"Harold, you mentioned your new understanding of something Christ said. I too have a great respect for your master Christian, Yeshua Ben Miriam."

"I was brought up as a Christian, but I've never heard the name Yeshua Ben Miriam, who was he?"

"He is your Jesus," Malkuth continued. "The Christians changed his real name Yeshua to Jesus when they translated his teachings from Aramaic, his language to Greek. Jesus is a Greek name, not Jewish, and I suspect why they did that was because at the time, the language of Hebrew was not popular or perhaps many Christians still blamed the Jews for killing their master and so the name Jesus is how he is now universally known. A name is not important, but he made many references to being present. Just before his arrest he spoke to his disciples, saying, 'Will you not stay awake with me for a single hour?' It was not sleep that he was referring to, but the endless jumping of our minds that lacks presence, ever seeks direction, purpose and value, that is attached to results."

"I had no idea that the name Jesus was not his original name. Knock me over with a feather. Anyway, please help me to remember these attachments more easily, Malkuth."

"Only your ego is afraid of not remembering this. Because perhaps it has made this wisdom into a value, yes?"

Harold, embarrassed, nodded.

"But if it helps in contemplation, what do you think are the main intellectual activities of the mind that are attachments and making something into a value or something less valuable through a judgment?"

"Well, comparing to start with. I do this all the time. Comparing how things should be according to my value system and beliefs, and when my expectations are not met, no wonder I have had so much anger in my life."

"What is the next thing people do that follows a comparison?"

"When I compare, and find that this situation is not to my liking, what I do then is.., I judge it as good or bad. So, judging is the second one, yes?"

"Indeed, yes. Then, what do you do?"

"I resist it because I have already judged it as bad. I resist it because I want to change it. I want it to be different, so I am going to war with it. Then what do I do? Don't tell me, I'm sure I can work it out as I remember the last time I was highly stressed.

"I start to look for a solution, yes, that's what I do. And of course, I look for a solution outside myself. I start to figure out how I can start feeling better again. So this attachment is.. is.. it's coming to me, analyzing, analyzing the problem to find a solution."

Harold looked at Malkuth for confirmation and his smile and slight nod encouraged him further. "There is another one, and it's ... Okay, stop trying, old boy it will come, just be here now and let it come. I got it! I lose myself in identifying myself with the belief or with the activity I'm engaged in. Or I lose myself in identifying with my thoughts, or my feelings or with the pain in my body. I think I am these things and therefore fall into suffering or being a victim."

Harold no longer needed verification from Malkuth as the inner knowing flowed through his whole being. As ego fell away, a gentle humility became present in him and he gently continued.

"The five attachments themselves are not the problem, but the unconsciousness of them operating in us is what separates people, not only from the present moment, but also from themselves, and then from each other. So, there is no wonder there are so many conflicts within people, between people and between nations."

"I will write them down, so I can more readily see when they are operating in me." said Harold.

COMPARING

JUDGING

RESISTING

ANALYZING

IDENTIFYING

He looked at what he had just written. "Yes, that's me alright. Well, at least these are my main mental behaviors and explain why I have so many values, so many attachments and why I am so unhappy whenever a value is being taken away or even threatened to be taken away and is enough to get me mad."

He was silent, as doubts started to creep in, which he could see was resistance to accepting a possible new reality or a resistance to change. He was with it. Then he spoke, still needing some reassurance.

"But honestly, Malkuth, is it really possible to live without attachments?"

"Without these five attachments there is only now. But I still see you have doubts and that is normal when a person has spent their whole life living from their attachments, so here is a question to ponder.

Is it possible for a value to exist without an attachment?" Harold closed his eyes to be more with the question, allowing intuition to bring the answer. After a long pause he opened his eyes and saw a new reality. "No, it's not possible." He heard himself say.

"How do I know it is a value unless I compare it with a non-value, a process that separates me from myself.

Malkuth cut in. "Of course, comparisons between something you want to do or have is innocent. It is only those comparisons that are based on strong beliefs about right and wrong or how the world should be that harbors fear, which triggers equally strong judgments and the cascade of the following attachments that separate us from the present moment.

Yet, and remember, these five attachments are not the problem, because there are no problems. The fact is that most people are not even aware that these things run their lives and therefore are not present with them. Then they learn about attachments and have discovered a new 'bad' guy in the neighborhood and ask, how can I live without them or how can I get rid of them? Notice that we are still into making them wrong. Attachments are not wrong, they just are. While we live with values we will continue to live inside attachments and outside ourselves. Before, people saw the bad guy was fear and now it's attachments and what do people do? They try to get rid of them, which is just another attachment.

"Being present is not about getting rid of our attachments. This is the most crucial point. The true inner work is not about trying to rid ourselves of anything but being present with them when they are operating. 'Resist not evil,' as so the master Christian said. That will cause them to fall away on their own, without us having to do a technique or learn a process or some collection of knowledge to become free of them. A person is already free when he or she is present with them.

And that is enough for today."

Harold started to stand in preparation to leave, saying, "I said before that this information will be shocking for intellectual people and I have to say how shocking it has been for me. I think this fifth tablet was written especially for me."

They both laughed.

Chapter Fifteen
Who do You Think You Are?

Marlene looked at the computer screen: there was no message from her father or Jonathan. Barbara, Marlene's friend holding her coffee, asked, "Still no word?"

"No, it's been nearly a week and I've heard nothing. Dad was very reassuring in his last message that everything was okay after the boat accident where they lost half of their equipment. But he's so much into this positive thinking stuff that he is often so unreal. I sometimes don't get Dad, but some highly inspirational quote about everything being better than better. I think I liked him more before he started all this 'rah rah, fake it until you make it' sort of approach to life. I feel he uses this to hide his feelings ever since Mum died and it puts a wall between us and it makes him seem false or something."

Barbara followed on, "I had an uncle like that and he was so positive all the time that it seemed unnatural. I mean, you do meet beautiful people who are genuine and positive, but you feel it's not an act, that they are genuine and honest and maybe it's because they are honest with how they feel. Anyway, my uncle died of heart disease in his early forties and my mother said to me that when you spent your life pretending to be someone you feel you are not, it can end up killing you."

"Yes, I think that is very similar to Dad. I remember when I was a little girl and before he was into all this jazzed up 'I'm a winner' jargon that he throws around, he was more real, and I really felt his love. I feel sorry for him because I love him so much. I think he's still carrying a lot of pain from Vietnam, and Mum's passing only added to it. Maybe tomorrow something will come from them. But probably not, because he did say that once their batteries ran out, communication would end and so I guess that has happened. I'm a bit scared, because if they were in trouble, Dad wouldn't mention it. I wish he was more honest with me."

Having completed meditation, Malkuth gently smiled at Harold as if to say, 'how are you?'

"This latest stone '**Who do you think you are**,' is really a strange title. This is an expression that people use in my country as an insult, suggesting that the person is arrogant or a know it all. It is not a flattering comment to make to a person, so I am completely puzzled by what this stone is saying. Then this morning I looked at it again from my feelings instead of intellect and it started to make some sense. So, I think it means I have a perception of myself, which is my self-image. Self image is the conclusions I form about myself from my upbringing and cultural conditioning, yes?"

"That is part of it, yes, go on, Harold."

So, if I have a low opinion of myself, I will try to create an ideal self, which I want to show to the world, which is my self- importance. I have realized for some time that in trying to build up my self esteem by being a better person, speaking more elegantly, dressing more fashionably, learning information and techniques to impress other people with my knowledge, looking good in the eyes of others, making myself more valuable that we spoke about yesterday, does nothing to my self esteem but builds self importance. That is why I rushed into all those positive thinking courses, believing that if I acted positively, it would make me into a more positive person. I remember this guy years ago running a seminar on self-esteem said that there was no difference between low self-esteem and high self-importance and they both supported each other in keeping a person in a state of unconsciousness. I didn't fully agree with him at the time, but now I think it is true."

"Probably is, Harold, go on."

"So, the tablet is saying that I think I am a certain way, or I think I am a certain person, but I am not any of these. Perhaps I am not a human being, having occasionally a spiritual experience, but a spiritual being having a human experience."

"When I read the slab a few minutes ago, Harold, I felt it was saying something deeper. What I'm hearing from you is more coming from your previous knowledge and therefore from the intellect. Try reading it again from your heart."

Harold picked up the slab and felt slightly disappointed that what he thought was a very sophisticated explanation hadn't seemed to have impressed Malkuth at all.

"This time when you read it, feel the words, don't think them, and feel them from the depths of your heart."

With his next reading, the feelings of inspiration, creativity and intuition again began to flow. Closing his eyes, he heard himself say, "Who I think I am, is not what or who I really am. Who I think I am, is a role or a function. I think I am my intellect, my thoughts, beliefs, attitudes, knowledge and motives. I think that my judgments are correct and that my values are the truth. That the world would be a better place if everyone thought like me. Such arrogance is lodged in the hidden corners of my mind.

He continued more confidently as the energy of presence expressed themselves through him. "I think I am my emotions. When I am angry, sad, jealous or glad, fearful or loving, I reinforce the belief that I am my feelings by saying, 'I am afraid, I am happy.' The words 'I am' something, not only reinforce this belief, but also establishes a distance from who I really am, through the process of identification with what I feel. The body, the mind, experience these emotions, but I lose myself in my feelings by calling them me.

"I think I am my body, especially if I have a tooth ache and say I am hurting. I have become identified with a part of the body that I think is the essential part of me, again through identifying with this body.

"I am only these things when I lose myself in identifying with them. I am not what I call my mind, nor am I emotions, nor am I this body, for they are but the instruments I use while on this plane of existence. They are no more than a function, a very useful function, I might add."

He paused, letting the information that had just passed his lips filter down into deeper levels of himself. The moment passed, and the inspiration, creativity and intuition were spent. He opened his eyes and Malkuth was in his usual prayer pose, when he was fully present with himself. Malkuth smiled at him and gently nodded.

"Listening to you, Harold, reminds me of the joys of being an assistant to such people as yourself. You covered the essentials of what the tablet speaks of. But, I suspect there are other forms of identification and you did briefly mention it, do you remember?"

"Yes, the roles that we play. Shakespeare wrote that the world is a stage and the people are the players, that we are all playing a role and then think we are the role; but I would be interested in more of your thoughts on the matter of identification, Malkuth."

"Let us assume that we have a true self that we can never know through the intellect, because the intellect is not a refined enough instrument to fathom the unknowable. As an infant we were more connected to our true self, that pure essence that knows no attachment; that simply lives purely from being present. As we grew, we had a constant input of other people's values, people who had lost contact with their own true selves. They taught us that we were capable of being good and bad and that certain things could be good and other things could be bad. That believing in this is good and believing in that is not good, that certain feelings could also be good and bad as well as behaviors. We learned duality, and this taught us separation. Because we loved these people we assumed that they were right and our then knowing of who we really are, got pushed away from us. Slowly, over the first seven years of a person's life the consciously knowing who we are, got transformed to what or who we **should** be. As we became more separate from the essence of ourselves, this was replaced with an artificial self, which could be called personality. Personality comes from the Greek word persona, which means mask. Personality is nothing more than a mask in order to emotionally survive in a world that is obsessed with the values of right and wrong and their accompanying attachments, that has no connection with the true self.

So, by the time we are an adult with all our knowledge, and with the regular practice of the five attachments, we are totally separated from our true self. Yet, this separation is only in consciousness and not in reality, because we can never be separated from what we are, any more than we could separate one part of the sky from another part. All is one. But the separation is nothing more than a case of forgetfulness. As we practice being present, the memories of our essence return.

We prevent ourselves from remembering by believing we are our functions and our roles. We identify with these things. Our identifications can reach further into groups. For example, if I am an atheist and now become a Buddhist or a Christian, have I changed my essential self, or have I simply changed my beliefs and identifications? You said before that you are a spiritual being having a human experience and that may be true, but how do you know? Maybe, because you learned it from somewhere, from some book perhaps. It may be another philosophy to identify with."

"My god, I'm full of philosophies, beliefs and systems. Please go on, Malkuth."

"The true self can never be defined by the intellect, because it is in the realm of the unknowable. Whenever people try to define the unknowable, such as the true self, truth or God, they limit the unknowable down to their own level of identification. Some groups even give their deity a personality, a gender and make it into a parental figure by calling it father. There is nothing wrong with this; it is merely the speaking of children and spiritual immaturity that is still seeking a parent to take care of them. They will eventually pass through this as they learn to be present with themselves.

"Let us make this more practical instead theoretical. Do you have a notebook and pen?"

Harold nodded.

"Good, then I will ask you a series of questions directly after each other, not giving you time to think and so write in your note book the very first thought that comes along in your mind. Just write down the very first thought. I will be asking in the first-person text, so it is a question directly to you, okay?"

Harold nodded again and sat with pen poised,

Malkuth started. "Who am I without my knowledge?

"Who am I without my values?

"Who am I without my beliefs?

"Who am I without my philosophies or religion?

"Who am I without my structures?

"Who am I without my career?

"Who am I without my money?

"Who am I without my possessions?
"Who am I without my family?
"Who am I without my country?
"Who am I really?
"Relax. What did you answer for each question?"
"My god, I'm just a mass of identifications, I'm full of them. With most questions I got 'I am nothing.' These things totally run my life. Is there any hope for me?"

"Harold, are you forgetting what we discussed yesterday? Having a life full of identifications is no problem. It is in trying to get rid of them. What will happen if you try to get rid of them, Harold?"

"I will get to keep them because I am making them wrong and that separation, that dualistic thinking of good and bad prevents me from being present with them."

"Yes. What did you answer for the last question?"
"I don't know who I am. Shit."

Malkuth gently smiled at Harold's humanness. "You are so down to earth, Harold, and you make many of your experiences very physical. Shit: you can't be more physical than that. No one knows who they are, for knowing is largely intellectual and being present has no aim to know or do anything. Of course, in living, doing is important, but we will discuss that later. I am pleased that you don't know who you are, Harold. That means you are going beyond the mind and starting to touch deeper levels. It also shows a healthy self-honesty.

It has been said that there is nothing new under the sun. Everything has already been said, experienced and written about. This is true when we live from our identifications. Everything is old, our thoughts, and knowledge and past experiences. But, when we start practising being present, then everything is brand new. Every experience is as if for the first time, every thought, feeling and action is unique, is like nothing that has ever happened before. Look at a flower, become one with the flower, flow with it, be fully involved and still be conscious of yourself. This is expanded consciousness that the intellect can never know. This ability cannot be learned from any book but discovered through the becoming present exercise.

"How did the being present exercise go for you since we met yesterday?"

"I did it three times. The first time quite well, but the second, I just became flooded with thoughts, so much so that I gave up in the end. The third time much the same as the second, so what am I doing wrong?"

"Harold, see what you just asked me, 'what am I doing wrong?' I'm not criticising what you are saying but pointing out your use of language, which reveals what we believe in. Can you hear what you just said?"

"What am I doing wrong, question? Yes, I'm still full of judgments about myself. I'm still very committed to the world of duality, of good and bad. Thank you for pointing that out. I will be more present with that. I'll say that again. Why was I having so many thoughts that were distracting me away from being present?"

"Your thoughts were neither the distraction nor even the judgment, but because of your unawareness and therefore your ability to be present with the judgment and the distraction. The key to being here now is in our awareness when we are not present. Being present isn't just about being with your thoughts, feelings and motives to act, but also includes anything that is taking you away from being present. Being with the attachment that is taking you away is being present. So, well done for seeing how you couldn't be present. When you are afraid, and you are present with being afraid, that is being present. With that presence the fear falls away by itself, without our having to do anything but simply be conscious of it. Nothing more is needed.

What we have discovered about attachments and especially about identification is that at our level of evolution, to be without them is impossible. This makes many people think that if this is the case then to be present is also impossible and this is not so. Being present when I see I am not present, is in fact, being present. And because we are absent most of the time simply catching ourselves in being absent, is being present. So, we have many opportunities to practise being aware.

Don't give up anything. Keep your fears, attachments addictions, but see them operating and be present at that moment and the attachment will then fall away. I have said that many times already and I will say it many times again in our work together, because it is the essence of what the tablets are saying. Anyone can be present when they are being loved and are happy, but the test of true presence is when everyone rejects us, including ourselves, when we are afraid, when everything is going against us. These are the times we need to pay attention to what is happening inside of us. This is the highest form of magic, because in this presence the whole universe begins to transform itself to our level of consciousness. Being present is when we see and feel that we are not present."

"Okay, I've got that, but there is something I still don't understand. Two days ago, when you first taught me the being present exercise, you said to be fully involved and not at a distance. I learned about objective consciousness and by observing events, thoughts and feelings as a witness, which was separating myself from a stressful situation in order to view it more objectively and therefore more consciously. But you were suggesting being fully involved with a thought, feeling and with my body; wouldn't that cause me to lose myself in that function through identification? That observing it objectively as a witness would be more effective?"

Malkuth replied. "Being the witness is a common practice among many groups. Being the witness and objective consciousness can only happen at integration. Integration is that state of consciousness when we are fully connected to all parts of ourselves in the present moment: when intuition is flowing through us and intellect is a faithful servant to it. Before integration, impartial observation is not possible. With every thought there will be an emotion and every emotion color the way we view things. Objective consciousness is only the result of waking up and it cannot be used as a technique to wake up. The original teachings of the witness correctly described the results of integration. But many less conscious people got hold of it and used it as a technique instead of using consciousness. What do you think will result if I try to be the witness and achieve objective consciousness, especially during an emotional crisis, when my thoughts are charged with high emotions?"

"My god, I will suppress my feelings. Oh shit, that is what I have been doing when I thought I was being positive and conscious. I was, in fact, escaping what I was really feeling. And this would lead me into being even more unconscious."

"Many people do not have a good relationship with their emotions and use the concept of the witness as a way not to feel them. Unfortunately, there is no neutral or impartial observation outside of integration, despite what all the numerous books and seminars say."

"Thank you, Malkuth, that does explain a lot, especially about not striving to get rid of attachments, because I have so many of them it would take me for the next million years. So here is a spiritual joke. Enlightenment is realising that I am not enlightened."

Smiling, Malkuth replied, "If it existed, that would be the closest to it, yes. Until tomorrow, dear friend!"

Chapter Sixteen
The unexpected

Helen was running towards him, her long blond hair streaming behind her. He was running towards her, his arms outstretched to receive her, and he could hear her laughter at the joy of their meeting. But when they were ten steps from each other, her face suddenly became fearful, wide-eyed with terror. She hesitated in her stride and her hand came up to cover her mouth.

Harold opened his eyes with a start and glanced at his watch, which said 04.45. "What a dream," he thought. Then, without warning, he saw a shadow reach out to him from the darkness, and a pair of rough hands were grabbing at him and dragging him out of his hammock, onto the floor. Then another pair of hands grabbed him, and he was unceremoniously dragged out of his tent and thrust against another body. He shook his head to see if he was still dreaming. A bright light shone in his eyes, blinding him, causing him to turn away from the glare.

"Are you okay, Dad?" came Jonathan's voice beside him on the ground. He sighed with relief that his son was okay. He reached out his hand and touched Jonathan's arm to reassure him. Jonathan climbed to his feet. A figure approached Jonathan and barked at him in a foreign language:

"Go take a running jump, you asshole!" Jonathan barked back. The man took a step closer and Harold recognized the martial arts move. Without warning, the man swung his leg in a reverse roundhouse kick, striking the side of Jonathan's head with his heel and down he went. Harold was at his side instantly. Jonathan shook his head. He seemed okay, but no doubt such a blow would cause some concussion. Harold looked back, his eyes now adjusted to the dark, and saw a short man, slim and very muscled. He silently named him, Tokyo Joe.

There seemed to be about six of them, and there was a lot of loud talking in Portuguese, and to Harold's shock he thought he heard Arizona's softly spoken voice among them. Next, Arizona knelt in front of Harold.

"Hello again! Where is it? Where is the treasure, Harold?"

"Arizona, the treasure is not what we all thought it would be. It is only a treasure of stones with writings on them and nothing more."

"Don't mess with me! These men are dangerous. They want to kill you and I have been arguing with them for days to leave you in peace once we have the treasure. Where is it?"

"It is in my tent in a large wooden chest, but I have told you, there is no treasure of gold or diamonds, just stone slabs."

Arizona slapped Harold, not too hard, but enough to startle him. "Where is the treasure, man?" he yelled in a rare display of frustration.

A large man standing beside Harold's tent spoke to Arizona in his language, no doubt asking him what Harold had said. Arizona turning to him, replied. The big man turned to someone who was ransacking Harold's tent and barked an order. A voice from inside called back that he had found the wooden chest. They heard him open it, then silence. The big man, who was obviously their leader, disappeared inside the tent. More silence. They then heard the wooden chest being overturned and the stone tablets clanking against each other as they rolled out of the chest and onto the ground. They could see several torches, what appeared to be frantically sweeping every corner of Harold's tent. A low growl of anger escaped from the tent and within seconds the big man was standing over Harold. He spoke in a low and threatening voice to Arizona.

"The chief says that if you don't tell us where the treasure is within the next ten seconds you are both to be shot. You are a good man, Harold. I don't want you shot, please tell us where the real treasure is, and no harm will come to you."

"Tell him that if we had a treasure we would gladly give it to him for our lives, but that is all there is, I'm sorry."

Arizona turned to the chief, saying in Portuguese, "He says that is all the treasure is, just those stones. I think he is speaking the truth."

"Then kill them for wasting our time," the chief spat out and turned to leave.

"No, don't do that, Chief," Arizona pleaded. "They mean no harm. Leave them be, Chief. You promised."

"I said kill them and if you can't find the treasure with the map you have, you will end up the same way."

The man who had kicked Jonathan, Tokyo Joe, laughed sneeringly at Arizona, saying, "You are lying. You are in league with them to get the treasure for yourself. You just wanted our help to capture them."

The Chief turned back towards Arizona and swung his fist against the back of Arizona's neck and he crumbled onto the ground next to Harold.

"Kill them all and that bastard Arizona, too, for wasting our time."

He turned and walked away, and two men with rifles stepped towards the three of them on the ground to carry out the chief's orders.

Harold looked around for an escape route or a means of diversion, but Arizona was unconscious, and Jonathan was concussed and unable to respond to anything he might do to save them. Harold's frantic thoughts were interrupted from the edge of the jungle with a loud, "Stop!"

The outline in the semi-darkness of a familiar figure stepped into the middle of the group. It was Malkuth. He seemed fearless and gently but firmly spoke to the chief in the man's own language. The chief respond with a small wave of his finger to the two men with rifles, who each grabbed one of Malkuth's arms. He did not resist or pull back, but instead with piercing eyes looked sharply at the man holding his left arm. His gaze was not aggressive nor hostile but had a power that the man had never seen or ever felt before, which caused him to let go and step back. Not so much from fear, but in confusion and amazement. Malkuth sharply turned to the man on his right and repeated the piecing stare, which also caused this man to let go and step back.

Tokyo Joe stepped towards Malkuth with a hostile and aggressive stance and was preparing to kick out at Malkuth, who looked back at him with the same look as he had given the other two men, causing him to stop in mid-track. The two men, standing two meters apart, eyed each other for seconds that seemed to everyone watching as an eternity. Some silent communication was travelling between the two men and everyone felt it. Tokyo Joe snatched a rifle from one of the men standing near and menacingly shook it and pointed it directly at Malkuth's stomach, yelling, "You are not the boss here! You do as I say!" Malkuth did not flinch or show any signs of fear but kept his focused gaze on Tokyo Joe. Harold was nearly passing out with fear at the thought that one of the most important people in the world for him right now might get shot in the next few seconds. Tokyo Joe slowly and deliberately brought the rifle up into his shoulder and pointed it into the middle of Malkuth's chest. Then slowly took the first pressure on the trigger. He was sweating, and his arms began to shake. He let out a piecing scream and fired.

Harold rolled onto the ground and moaned in utter despair, "Oh no, please god no!" From the angle he was lying, he couldn't see much except for a lot of smoke from the rifle blast and as it started to clear, Malkuth was still standing as if nothing had happened. Harold saw the rifle muzzle pointing to the ground and Tokyo Joe hysterically laughing at his joke of pretending to shoot Malkuth and suddenly moving the rifle down in the last split second. Malkuth again had not flinched, nor even stepped back. He remained silent and kept looking as if he were looking into the shorter man's soul and finally this was too much for Tokyo Joe and without taking his eyes off Malkuth, yelled to the rest of the gang. "We are wasting our time here! Let's go and find some real treasure."

The chief nodded and called to his men. "Let's go." Pointing to Arizona and not realizing that he was still unconscious, said "If I ever see you again you're dead meat. Do you hear me?"

As quickly as they arrived they disappeared into the jungle. Malkuth turned also to leave and said to Harold calmly, as if nothing had happened, "See you again at midday." The jungle also swallowed him up.

Harold sat on the ground beside Jonathan and Arizona in shock at what had just taken place in a matter of a few minutes. Jonathan started to come too at the same time as Arizona started moaning and rubbing the back of his neck and then opening his eyes. Looking around him in a daze, he mumbled, "Oh ouch, what happened? Where are those bad men?"

Then, embarrassed, looking at Jonathan and Harold, he continued, "I am sorry about what happened with me stealing the stone map and bringing those bad men here. They were not friends of mine and they assured me that they would not harm you. Your talk of buried treasure got the better of me. Please do not punish or report me. I made a mistake and I will make it up to you if you give me the chance."

Jonathan, shaking his head as if to get some clarity with his thoughts, responded first. "What happened? How come those guys are gone?"

Arizona started to talk, and Harold cut in. "That was noble of you to try and save our lives and made what you did forgivable and," looking at Jonathan, "We were saved by Malkuth and I'll tell you more about that shortly." Looking back at Arizona, he said "How long have you been trying to find us and how did you find out about the stone map?"

"I am going to tell you the whole truth; hide nothing from you. Again, I am so sorry."

Harold waved his hand for him to stop apologizing and get on with the sorry.

"Okay, thank you. After our first meeting in Manaus, I followed you back to your hotel and was able to get a room next to yours. I suspected that you were not archaeologists and I was able to hear you both talking about a treasure map. The walls were not thick. I contacted this gang who agreed to help me get the treasure and we agreed to split it, two-thirds to them and one third to me. They said they would kill you once they got the treasure, but I said the deal was off if they harmed you in any way. I was a fool to trust them on this. They probably would have killed me as well if the treasure was real. Anyway, they were not good men and they were not good in the jungle either. But they followed along after us by half a day and then you, Harold, left an easy trail for them with your colored ribbons. The night I left after stealing the stone with the map, I made my way back the way we had come and met up with them. I brought them back to your campsite a day later and then tracked you for the next three days. I found the site and the hole where the treasure was buried. Not from the stone map, as I couldn't understand that at all, only by tracking you. Then I lost you at one of the rivers."

Jonathan glanced in Harold's direction, "So your special forces trick worked, eh Dad?"

Arizona continued, "I guessed by that stage you were an experienced bushman and it took me a long time to finally pick up your tracks after exploring both sides of the river for several miles in both directions. It cost us three more days and the gang were no help. They couldn't track an elephant in a patch of mud, so I had to do it all on my own, which is why it took me so long. I was worried that the rains would wash all signs away, but the mule tracks mostly gave you away, and so it wasn't difficult once you left the river. Finally, I was able to track you to here. I found Henry's body, or his skeleton. The ants make quick work of anything that dies, and I recognized it was Henry because it was bigger-boned. I'm sorry. I know how dear he was to you both."

"So," Harold asked, "you did not go ahead to try and find the treasure before us then after all?"

"No."

"That is amazing, because I thought I saw your track by the river and that caused us to go south in a large loop instead of the western route that I thought you were taking. My god, some animal must have left it and if that hadn't happened we would never have found the Beacon. That is truly amazing."

"Do you still have the tablet with the map?" Jonathan asked.

Arizona pulled it out from his small backpack and handed it to Jonathan.

"Look here, Dad. That carved line towards the Beacon with the arrow on it is pointing due east. That means it was as we mentioned once and dismissed it, but it was the only possible route that would enable us to find the Beacon." Bringing his hand to his forehead in wonder, he continued "If that animal, which probably passed that spot minutes before we arrived, hadn't broken that leaf off the tree, we would have continued on our southerly route and would never have found the treasure at all."

"So, there is a treasure after all?" Arizona asked hopefully.

Harold replied, "Not quite. The stones that your friends found in my tent are the treasure and what a treasure they are, yes indeed. They are the treasure of the most amazing wisdom I could have ever dreamed of in a million years. The gentleman who arrived and saved us all has been helping me decipher the ancient writings. So, from your perspective, there is no real treasure, but from mine it has been what I have been searching for my whole life."

"I am very pleased for you, Harold. With your forgiveness, I will refund your complete guide fee and I leave my shotgun with you as a gift. I have about thirty shots for it and will return to Manaus." He handed Harold a belt of cartridges for the shotgun and a business card, "Here is my personal address in Manaus. You are both invited to come and stay with me and my family for as long as you wish. I did a bad thing and so you come and let me repay you with my hospitality for my foolishness. I put both your lives in danger and that was never my intention. I am sorry."

Harold took the liberty of putting his arm around Arizona's shoulder and affectionately said, "Dear man, your actions did put us in danger, that's true, but without your part in all this by taking the map, we would never have found the site within a million years. I don't understand any of it, but one thing is becoming clearer: without a whole string of events and your sudden departure at exactly that time, that animal leaving a mark, Henry breaking his leg and all the other things, well, we wouldn't have found anything. Somehow all these events have been part of some master plan that led us to the site. Arizona, you were a vital part of the puzzle. Thank you for your part in it, and besides, there is no need to refund us the guide's fee."

"Wait a minute Dad…"

Harold held up his hand to stop Jonathan from speaking further, saying to Arizona, "You are welcome to stay with us." On seeing Arizona shake his head, he continued, "Will you have breakfast with us before you leave?"

"What happened. Who saved us? Jonathan muttered.

"It was your Malkuth who saved us. Did you see him, how he dealt with those guys?"

"Who saved us was Malkuth, the guy you go and see every day, your teacher friend?"

"Yes, and he was so amazing."

"I didn't see him as I must have been unconscious from the kick in my head."

"Did you say his name was Malkuth?" Arizona cut in. Harold nodded.

"When I was a young man, I attended a lecture by a Professor of Ancient History and he told us some historical facts that few know about, and that has been largely lost in the passing of time to end up being a legend. It was of a great spiritual teacher called Malkuth. The legend says that he was the author of a special wisdom that was carved onto twelve tablets of stone, but that Malkuth must have died over 1500 years ago. He was the great father of the Aztec people, which is why they flourished so well and for so long. Then something happened, perhaps their great leader left, and the wisdom was lost, and it is reported that the people fell into savagery and human sacrifice. But you said, Harold, that the treasure is stone tablets. May I see them?"

They made their way to Harold's ransacked tent and there were the tablets strewn over the tent floor. Harold noted that his revolver and holster were still lying under his hammock and was surprised that the bandits had missed them. It was starting to get lighter as the sun was beginning to rise. Arizona bent down and took one of the stones in his hands. He nodded to himself.

"This is amazing. I don't know for sure, but they seem to be the very same lost stone tablets that the legend talked about, and, according to the professor, have not been seen for over a thousand years."

Jonathan interrupted with a proud note in his voice, "And my father can read them."

Arizona looked at Harold, "You can read these?"

"Well, not entirely. Malkuth is helping me to understand them. We are meeting for several hours each day."

"Your Malkuth can read these?" Arizona asked again in mounting excitement.

"And you can too, Dad." Jonathan insisted. Harold modestly shook his head, while Arizona looked carefully and concentrated with all his consciousness for about 10 seconds and then gave up. "I can't read them. The professor said that the only ones who can read and understand them were enlightened masters." Looking carefully at Harold, he said "Perhaps you are an enlightened master, mister Harold?"

"I don't think so. I don't understand them so that rules me out if your professor was right, but I think Malkuth is."

Arizona continued, "Your mister Malkuth is either the original immortal Malkuth that the professor spoke of, or he is the reincarnation of the original, or he is a great teacher who took the same name. If he can read and understand these stone tablets, whoever he is, then for sure he is an enlightened being."

Chapter Seventeen

Beware of your benefactor

Harold seated himself opposite Malkuth and looked at him through different eyes. Who was this man really, he thought? Malkuth smiled back at him.

"How is Jonathan after taking such a blow to the side of his head?

"He is okay, but he has many questions about you."

"Perhaps it is you that has the many questions. How is Arizona? He took quite a blow to the back of his neck."

"He is okay as well and has left to return home." He paused, not sure of how to word the next question. "You seem to be aware of everything that happens, so, I have to ask, did you know yesterday that Arizona and the gang of bandits were going to attack us last night?"

"Yes."

"Why didn't you warn me yesterday?"

"If I'd warned you, you and Jonathan would have been on the alert."

"Exactly! And we could have been ready for them."

"Had you been ready for them Harold, people would have surely got hurt and even killed and I have a special interest in two of those men as I will probably be working with them in the future if certain things come to pass."

"You are going to work with two of those cut-throats?"

"I am going to work with two of those men, one of them is the person you named as Tokyo Joe. I will probably be working with him in five years' time."

"But he nearly killed you!"

"Yes, he did and that would have altered a great many things, especially for him."

"And for me too! For heaven's sake, were you not afraid of dying?"

Looking at Harold as if it was a very strange question, he said, "Why would I be afraid of something that does not exist until it happens?"

"You mean, you don't carry the fear of death, at all?"

"Let us say, that when one is in the present moment there is no fear, because there are no judgments, or beliefs that can generate fear. Also, in the present moment there is no time. There is always now. Everything else is an illusion. For example, 5 minutes from now does exist except in someone's expectation. 5 minutes ago, equally does not exist except in someone's memory."

"So," Harold asked, "if there is no time in the here and now, which means no passage of time, if we lived here permanently, would we age, or would it be possible to live indefinitely, say for at least 1500 years, yes?"

Malkuth was silent, then spoke. "This is not the time to speak of such intricate details of time in the present moment. You will find your own answer in due course as you practice living here now."

Harold thought to himself, 'He's avoiding any question that hints at him being a master. Interesting!'

"Okay and I have another question, may I?" Receiving Malkuth's nod, he continued, "I asked you six days ago if Arizona was close and you said no. Yet, you knew that the bandits were going to attack us last night. How did you know all these things?"

"That is simple to explain. We are all one and therefore connected in consciousness. When we are fully present, then that oneness is made conscious and to know what another person thinks, feels and experiences is not difficult."

"So, there could have been a different outcome last night if we were prepared."

"Indeed, it would have been."

"So," Harold contemplated, "Nothing in destiny is fixed, then?"

"There is a general plan for every person to realize their full potential. And the general direction is augmented by a person's thinking, beliefs, personality and other influences. Basically, an open book of destiny that can be changed with a different choice and decision in any given moment to go there or not to go there, to do this or not to do that and so on. Life is really an open book of potential possibilities, but there are no accidents. Cause and effect, except in the present moment where a person's willpower commands."

"You said that if Tokyo Joe had killed you, that would have altered many things for him, but how would that have affected you, and my reality as well?"

"Well, in fact, Harold, I was not in any real danger."

"No? It didn't look that way to me. If he'd not lowered the rifle in the split second before firing, surely you would not be here now, right?

Malkuth smiled as he looked at his friend and replied. "No, I would still be here. Let me explain. Simply by being fully present with one's thoughts, feelings and body and then in the stillness of that integrated state, make a conscious choice and any desired outcome one may have will be manifested."

Harold felt the growing excitement in him as he found something he could completely relate to.

"So, are you saying that simply choosing to be safe is enough to be safe, which means that choosing to be positive does really work, then?"

"No. You are missing the most important element, Harold. You need to be fully present first. Many people using positive thinking or what some call creative visualization to imagine some desired outcome is like using one tiny fragment of their power, which is why such techniques rarely work. They are not present with themselves and are using a small part of their creativity to escape an unwanted self or to change something they don't like in themselves. In this case there is little presence.

There are various levels of being present. The first one is where most people start their journey by first seeing how their fears, their attachments and beliefs run them. Then as they make their three functions more conscious, their levels of presence increase because the further three functions of the true self get activated. You remember what they are?"

"Yes, creativity, inspiration and intuition."

"Yes, and these get turned on, in a small way for those new to the journey, but, as one practices the exercise and practices in everyday life, especially during a crisis, they start to become more and more crystallized in one's being. As their awareness connects more and more with creativity, inspiration and intuition, they become more integrated and more connected to all their powers. Eventually, to be fully conscious, fully integrated, and then, making a conscious choice and decision for something to happen that you desire, will start to make it happen. For those with a lot of present-moment practice, it can happen almost instantly. This is the power of the white magician, the ancient alchemist and present-day experienced practitioners of conscious presence. When we are fully present, the power behind every thought and feeling is released. The power is there in every person but is never realized because of the lack of presence. This means in this integrated state, whatever you think about instantly begins to manifest. In the state of being here now, your thoughts become one with reality and in that oneness, creation happens."

"I can imagine it must take a lot of time and practice to reach this level of awareness to manifest a thought onto the physical plain, like you did last night with those bandits, I mean those men."

Malkuth paused as to find the most effective words. "Technically, no. The second a person enters the present moment; all their powers are open to them instantly. But because most people believe in limitations, don't trust their powers or lack the knowledge of even having them, or feel less about themselves, also get manifested on the physical plain, and so are prevented from fully entering the here and now.

"So, the key behind all power lies in being present?" Malkuth nodded.

"I am starting to see the limitation of contrived positive thinking. People practice positive thinking to become more conscious, but it only works when people practice being more conscious first, then positive thinking naturally happens. In fact, forced positive thinking would take people in the opposite direction of themselves. It has been such a big thing in the human potential movement, but hardly anyone ever talked about being present, while they did their creative visualizations and positive affirmations. Thank you for that explanation."

Malkuth continued. "The power behind people's thoughts when they are not present is very small, which is just as well, because humanity would have destroyed itself long before now, because of the amount of fear each person carries.

But enough of this conversation about integrated states, as it can easily drift into becoming another aiming point or yet another philosophy of spiritual knowledge that feeds the ego." "But, you are not against knowledge, techniques and philosophy about high states of consciousness?"

"I am not against these or anything else. Everything has its place. But when we use these things in place of consciousness, we separate from ourselves. All things that originate from outside of us, have the tendency to color our perception by forming into beliefs, which eventually turn into attachments that we talked about yesterday. Then we use them in place of being present and lose sight of who we really are. Anything that originates from outside of us has the potential to inspire us, which has turned on the true self, but unless we are present with it, the inspiration can fall back into an emotional high, which is the same as excitement. Excitement can be an ego trick to deny feelings of unconscious fear. When we practice being present in life and with the exercise, then every part of us turns into the direction of the true self and consciousness naturally expands.

But let us proceed with the next stone. Can you read it, Harold?"

"Yes, but again I have no understanding what it means. '**Beware of your benefactor.**'"

"What is a benefactor, Harold?"

"I guess someone who supports me, who gives me a benefit."

"Like a teacher?" Malkuth, added.

"I'm sure the stone is not referring to anyone like you, Malkuth."

"And why not? Do you regard me as a teacher, as a benefactor?"

"Yes, but why would I need to be, let's say, to be on my guard against you? But, can I interrupt this conversation with a question that I simply must hear from your own lips, who you truly are? Arizona thinks that you are an enlightened master and I think he is right, is that true?"

Malkuth was silent and looked back at Harold, but his face revealed nothing.

"I can see why you don't understand the seventh stone. This is the major step of responsibility in the journey of a developing being. It is not always an easy step to take for many.

Harold, every time you make me bigger than you, you make yourself smaller. The age of the guru, enlightened master or savior is past. It was needed before this time when humanity thought of itself as a child needing a parent. To this point humanity was vulnerable and immature needing that guidance of a loving caretaker. In the past the relationship between priest and follower, church and worshiper, guru and student, required the following of certain important rules and in a sense, obedience. A person couldn't command others or themselves until they had learned to obey. Certain guidelines needed to be followed to experience the deeper levels of the true self that was described then as divine or the grace of God.

"But that time is gone, to be replaced with the practice of being present. Now with the new energy coming onto the planet of self-responsibility and spiritual maturity, if a spiritual leader or guru demands obedience it will reinforce the hierarchy of values. Such values, religion, science were all an important part of human development and evolution, and were the driving force to grow, achieve, love and move towards what we really are. Even though 95 percent of the earth's population is still there, the age of the intellect, knowledge and information is passing to be replaced by the age of intuition, the age of conscious presence. Once these old values were essential and now they are more and more becoming atavistic, obsolete and a trap for both student and guru.

The Age of Being Present corresponds with your Age of Aquarius that you learnt in one of the seminars you attended, Harold, which is the time when humanity assumes the role of its own spiritual responsibility, where each person becomes their own guru, teacher or spiritual master. Not in name, which can impress the ego, but in consciousness. This is the stage of stepping out from the shadow of the parent and assuming responsibility for oneself and in a sense becoming their own parent, their own master."

"What did you mean: not in name but in consciousness?" Harold asked.

Some people reach this stage of waking up in consciousness but are still controlled by ego. They learn some spiritual truths, being often charismatic, which attracts people to them and the group feeds their self-importance, leading them to believe that they are enlightened. They are still living in the old world of needing a parent and so they make themselves into a parent to guide others. It is a difficult phase to see in oneself that many go through until they eventually find their inner presence. This phase can delay their journey for a while until the person learns humility and self-honesty, essential ingredients, especially self-honesty, in the practice of being present. This is not making gurus or masters wrong but explaining a process that happens to many who have some experience in being present but have temporarily fallen under the spell of their own ego.

A truly enlightened master is the peasant farmer who lives mostly in the present of his love, joy and inner freedom, and has no need to prove his wisdom to the world. He or she has great self-honesty about when they are not present with themselves. Self-honesty is not making oneself wrong, but simply telling the truth to oneself about their own thoughts and motives, feelings and behaviors.

"The great master Christian, Yeshua Ben Miriam never called himself a master nor the son of God, but the son of man. Perhaps there have been some statements that suggested he thought of himself as a master, but being familiar with his work, I am sure that such references were misquoted from his original words. Besides, among his best friends were prostitutes and tax collectors, who were regarded as the lowest level of society in his time. He never made himself greater than any other because he knew he was no better, and that the only difference was that he could see further. Like the person standing on the top of the mountain is no better than the person standing in the valley. Only the vision is different and their state of happiness and that is all. He even said that many would come after him who would do far greater things. He saw himself as a messenger and not the message. All too often a messenger is made into the message and a new value is born at the loss of presence.

So, Harold, look at the stone again, what do you understand about it now?"

"Before going on, can I please ask you a question or repeat a question that you didn't answer before and I promise never to ask anything about this again. Are you the original Malkuth who authored these twelve stone tablets?"

Malkuth's expressionless look returned. "What would change between us if you knew the answer, one way or another? What in you wants to know this answer?"

"Probably my ego. Probably because I want to figure you out."

"Perhaps to put me in a box of your understanding; perhaps to be able to say one day that your knowledge of presence was from a certain person, to give yourself creditability and self belief?"

"Yes, I think so, Malkuth. I have never believed much in myself and always looked to others for inspiration and guidance. Their opinions were always more important than my own and I can see that is where I am coming from now."

Malkuth softened. "Harold, I love your self-honesty. That is why I enjoy working with you. The practice of being present has no interest in origins of a wisdom or past histories, other than to be present with past experiences, by bringing them into the now. Whether I am the author of the twelve stone tablets or not has no bearing on our work together. Let us not speak of it again. What is important in what you last said was how you still looked to others for inspiration and guidance and that their opinions were always more important than your own. What does that tell you about our relationship?"

"That I have set you up as a guru, no, a parent. Oh shit. I'm as unconscious as everyone else."

Malkuth smiled. "With a big difference; you know you are unconscious and that knowing alone expands your awareness. So, look at the stone again," and, winking at him, asked, "What do you understand about it now?"

Harold expanded himself into his feelings in his usual way of being present with the stones, and within seconds his consciousness expanded further and allowed his intuition to flow through him.

"'**Beware of your benefactor...**' I now understand, it is not you that I need to be on my guard against, but something in me that is setting you up as a parent; that part of me that is afraid and looking for safety in others. That part of me that still thinks of itself as a child and wants to be loved, wants to be safe, wants someone to take my hand and reassure me, to carry me and to do it all for me.

Many cover this up by believing that they are confident, independent and powerful, which is hiding in the intellect. Others lose themselves in a philosophy or a leader to follow."

Harold was silent as he let the wisdom of his discovery of needing external authorities penetrate him.

Malkuth gently added, "There is nothing wrong in being a child, it means that a person remains with childish benefits, which are getting substitutes for love and avoiding pain and can only grow so far and not beyond. They have limited themselves only to that level. That is what a child does, but eventually every person grows up and will discover more of themselves." "Thank you again for this wonderful gift of understanding. I remember reading a book many years ago called, 'If you meet the Buddha on the road, kill him.' I didn't really understand what the author was on about back then, but now I realize this was the very thing he wrote about. **Beware of your benefactor,** not the benefactor him/herself but the unconscious choice to remain spiritually an infant. Wow, this is big stuff! I am not sure if much of the world is ready for this."

"Perhaps, perhaps not, but in time, this seventh stone may will be common knowledge and many people will be living it, along with the other eleven stones. While, others will take longer to step through their fears."

Smiling, Malkuth changed the subject and again winked at him, adding, "There is so much joyful information that is passed in such a small movement of one eye. You could use it more with Jonathan. I am happy to see you enjoying your times with him. You have been far too serious with him over the years. He remembers you most in how you played with him while he was a child. You were much more fun to be with when he was young, and you are returning more to that. And he will remember you with great love from these special times you are spending with him now. Cherish it yourself."

"And I'll make a value out of it," Harold said winking back at Malkuth; and they both laughed.

Chapter Eighteen
Being and doing, the two great powers lead you home

Jonathan was silent, and Harold detected some untypical restlessness in him.

"Are you okay, Jonathan?"

"Dad, have you noticed that since living in the jungle and being so close to nature that your senses are becoming more, how should I put it, more sensitive, more attuned to the environment?"

"Yes, but I put it down to the amazing work that I'm doing with Malkuth. So, you are feeling more connected, more grounded as well?"

"Yes, and I've noticed something else. I didn't want to say anything, but remember that story you told me when I was a teenager about when you were in Vietnam and you suddenly felt something was menacingly looking at you?"

"Go on," Harold replied.

"Well, yesterday, while swimming I felt something, or someone was watching me. But it didn't feel menacing as you described in your experience, and probably in that moment a sniper was probably trying to get you in his sights. Mine was different. But for about half an hour I felt some eyes looking at me. I didn't feel afraid, but I did feel weird. I got out of the water, grabbed the revolver and did a walk right around the outside of the camp, but there was nothing. Then as suddenly as it started it stopped. So maybe it's just my imagination or I still have some fears that those cut-throats might come back."

"Jonathan, you are pretty intuitive, so it probably was something, but I am sure if it was someone with ill intent or some predator animal like a jaguar, you would have felt a warning signal inside of you. I haven't felt any such feelings. Perhaps it was just a monkey or some such animal that was curious about human beings close to where it lives. But, keep an eye out just in case. I'm off to my appointment with Malkuth."

When Harold arrived at the meeting place with Malkuth, he was nowhere to be seen, so he sat down on the carpet in his usual place and started meditating. After about thirty minutes, still Malkuth had not arrived. Harold's curiosity about how Malkuth lived and what his camp site might look like kept coming to him. He stood up and made his way towards the area that Malkuth disappeared to each day to make a cup of tea at the end of their meetings. He followed a track for about thirty yards until he saw a large cave entrance in the side of a steep hill. The track led inside the cave, so he followed it. He entered a large cavern and he could see that there was an entrance into another cavern where a light was burning. He looked around in the semi darkness of the first cavern and could make out a fire hearth still glowing from recent use, with a stack of wood neatly packed beside it. Nearby, also neatly stacked, were cooking utensils, spotlessly clean. There was no furniture, but several cushions made from expensive-looking silk with startling colors were stacked neatly against one wall. The floor was covered with the same rich carpet that was outside at their meeting place. The atmosphere was dry and yet cool compared with the searing heat outside. Strings of herbs hung down from stakes protruding from the wall and ceiling. It was Spartan, yet homely and appeared very comfortable.

"Hello, Malkuth." he called, but there was no answer.

He cautiously moved towards the second cavern where the light was shining from. On entering it, he saw an equally large cavern as the first, also the floor covered with carpet and no furniture. There were candles burning from several different points and Malkuth was sitting in meditation at the far end. Without opening his eyes, he waved his arm for him to join him. Harold sat down opposite his friend and looked around at what could be described as the most perfect and comfortable home that could ever be made out of a cave. He could not see any other passageway or a sleeping place in either cavern and assumed that he must sleep somewhere else.

"Good afternoon, Harold. I wondered how long it would take you to get curious and come and find me."

"Afternoon, Malkuth. I hope you don't mind me making my own way into this most beautiful cave I have ever been in."

"You are most welcome. Are you ready to begin?"

"Ah, yes, and I have a question about the stones, all of them actually. They originated from the Aztec people, yes?" Malkuth nodded.

"How is it that such an amazing wisdom was born from a race that was so barbaric with their human sacrifices and unspeakable cruelty?" Harold asked.

"For one thing, these stones were carved long before the Aztec civilization existed. And another thing: who do you think were the first to record the history of the Aztecs?"

"Umm, I guess the Spanish did."

"And perhaps they wrote it from their own perspective, maybe from some agenda, who knows?"

"What do you mean, from some agenda?"

"What do you think were the objectives of the Spanish when they first arrived in South America?"

"To gather another colony and to obtain wealth for Spain. Oh yes, and to convert the people to Christianity, I guess."

"What better way than to paint a picture of barbarism to justify their actions to the outside world than by converting a race to a more humane and compassionate civilization, according to them."

"Are you saying, Malkuth, that the Spanish possibly made up those stories to further their own interest in spreading their rule as well as Christianity?"

"No, but I observe human motivation carefully and whenever a person or group is passionate about their beliefs that borders on fanaticism, they often feel justified in using any means available to further their aims. Perhaps their agenda was not so noble, but very successful. After all there is little evidence to the contrary, other than what the Spanish reported, that is left of what was once a great civilization that was probably wiser than the Spanish were themselves. We will never know, but I don't take seriously any person's reported account that is motivated by strong beliefs. Motivation, which is intellectual, is not always wise. Inspiration coming from intuition can never have a hidden agenda, as it is coming directly from the true self."

"Good lord, it never occurred to me that a whole history could have been fabricated to impose a different set of beliefs! I wonder how many times that has happened throughout human history?"

"I did not say that this happened in this country; but at the same time, I do not take seriously the Spanish written account of barbarism among the indigenous people, considering that there is no evidence of such in existence. Perhaps what was reported as sacrificial altars were instead altars of worship, no different in any Christian church today."

Harold carried on the thread of the conversation, saying, "Perhaps many of the modern-day religions have had their own agendas and did not always act nobly to ensure that their particular brand succeeded over others." Looking at Malkuth curiously, he said, "I think you know more than you are admitting to me about this and probably about many things.

Do you think the competition that exists in all the different religions is people pushing their own agendas and is coming from fear?" Before Malkuth could answer, he continued, "I am beginning to think that any form of competition is fear-based and certainly not love-based. What do you think?"

"What does it matter? What probably does matter is what do you feel about that?"

This question stopped Harold in his tracks as it sank in. "What I feel about it is some irritation at people's attempts at manipulating the truth to satisfy their own view point. In fact, that makes me angry."

"Seeing other people's motivations is useful. Seeing our own is even more useful. But being with what I feel about other people's and my own motivations is the most useful of all. Would you agree, Harold?"

"Oh, yes and thank you for stopping me to get so carried away. I have found your encouragement to be with my feelings and to read the tablets not from my intellect but from my heart the most amazing experience, thank you for that."

"And now, the eighth stone, would you care to read it out loud, Harold?"

"**Being and doing, the two great powers lead you home.** Again, I understand the words, but I'm a little unsure of the meaning."

"What in you, Harold, is the doing part?"

"The doing part of me I would suppose to be acting, behaving, achieving, discovering, umm..."

"Yes, and what name would you put on such qualities as these that is different to being?"

"Masculine quality, yes?"

"Yes and how would you describe the masculine quality?"

"I belonged to a men's group for a while and that was one of the best things I ever did. Masculine qualities are, let me think, are thinking, conscious mind, intellect, dynamic action and achievement, courage, to name just a few."

"You have a lot of masculine energy, Harold, but you also have a lot of feminine energy. A beautiful woman lives inside of you just waiting to express herself. However, these two qualities have nothing to do with gender, but simply two different energies that every person has. The conditioning of society has attributed them to a certain gender and when people do that, they get lost in gender identification."

"What is gender identification?" Harold asked.

"It is believing that you are a particular gender instead of it being a mere function or role. Men generally see themselves as men and very different to women, and women see themselves in the same way. Gender only exists in this field of existence and to assist souls into this plane. Yet millions of books have been written that carefully explain the differences as being real. Of course, there are obvious differences physically, hormonal and chemical functions, but in the very essence of each gender, beyond the physical, emotional and mental states, beyond the superficial coverings, there are no differences. The true part of each person, beginning with creativity, inspiration and intuition, both genders are the same. Gender identification has given rise to inequality, domination of one sex over another and even sex abuse. Both genders feel love and fear, both want the same things. There is no real difference between the genders and only millions of years of mental conditioning have created people to be so identified with their particular role.

"Perhaps read the stone tablet again, but this time read it from your heart, not your head."

Adjusting himself, his consciousness and holding the eighth stone in both hands, he started speaking, as Malkuth took up his usual position of resting his head on the points of his fingers.

"**Being and doing, the two great powers lead you home.** The two great powers are masculine and feminine, doing and being. The great energy of the masculine is doing and the great energy of the feminine is being, being receptive, open, and emotional, and the subconscious mind. The masculine asks the question from the intellect, and the feminine directs the answer through the feelings to intuition, which is the equal balance of both powers. Most people do not use these two great powers, which can be seen in a world that is at war with itself through international conflict, crime, poverty, disease and unhappiness. People think too much and feel too little, and this makes humanity act unnaturally, brutally and machine-like, thus preventing the world from seeing beyond its limited vision. The integration of the two energies is a great power that leads one home."

He stopped and absorbed what he had just said.

"My god, almost every level of society encourages the use of the intellect and discourages people from being emotional, which is looked upon as a form of weakness. I also never really considered myself as a man having feminine energy."

"Remember, it is not about gender, Harold, it is about qualities and every man on the planet has an equal amount of feminine inside of them as the women do and vice versa. The stereotype conditioning that most people get during those first seven important years of being here, trains them to deny the other half of who they are. Boys must wear blue, girls pink, boys should not cry or feel afraid and girls are allowed to feel afraid, but must never get angry. Only boys can do that because then they are expressing their maleness. This type of conditioning was the origin of chauvinism, which is making one sex greater or lesser than the other. And it is not just a male condition. Woman have their brand of chauvinism also by making themselves smaller through obedience to their husbands or seeing men as primitive or inferior to themselves. This denying of their other half is the real chauvinism in each person, and this has the tendency to suppress this part of themselves, creating imbalance in their energies and the expression of these energies.

"What happens in a person's life when they are out of balance and expressing too much masculinity with their feminine energy suppressed?"

"I suppose aggression, war, crime, violence, yes?"

Malkuth nodding, "Yes, and what happens when a person is expressing too much feminine energy and is not connected with their masculine to be in balance?"

"I guess a person would get lost in their feelings, confused and prone to fall into depression."

"Yes, Harold, but more to the point is that nothing happens. The person is stuck in their feelings and has not the willingness to do anything about it. The person is in a stagnant condition. Both energies are vital for our continued evolution. Unfortunately, as you pointed out, almost everyone on the planet is not in balance with these two vital energies and therefore does not experience their true power."

"I thought male energy was powerful and feminine energy was gentle."

Smiling at Harold, Malkuth continued, "Power is not a masculine quality, although most men think it is. Such a so-called power is having power over others through dominance and control and this is not true power, but aggression coming from fear. The three most afraid men of the twentieth century were Hitler, Stalin and Mussolini. They were so afraid that they had to surround themselves with huge armies and tried to conquer the world, because they had no control over themselves. They were so stuck in their masculine energies.

"So, what is true power? It is the ability and the willingness to act or not to act. Ability is a feminine quality, a quality that is being-ness without having to prove anything. Choice is another feminine quality. A choice to do this or that is energy in potential. On its own it cannot move nor do anything. The willingness is the will to do, to make a decision is masculine. Here is the dynamic action to move, achieve and do. Here the decisions are made based upon the available choices and a follow-through with action. Both qualities are needed to experience and express one's power. Both sides are needed in balance in being and doing."

"It all makes sense, but I have a question. If we focus more on our feelings as you are suggesting, is there a danger that we become so emotional, that our feelings start to run us?"

"A good question, Harold, emotional people are run by their feelings because they are not present with them. There is no suggestion here to favour emotions more than the intellect. Both functions are necessary and need to be balanced. People are either run by their feelings or by their intellect, not only because they are not present with them, but also because they are not balanced in between. Yet, the imbalance has been mainly caused by a lack of presence in a person. An emotional person needs to be more attentive to their feelings and also think more about their motivations and be present with both things. Intellectuals need to be more attentive to how their thoughts are running them and also to feel more and be present with each centre."

"Wow, I love what you are saying. It makes so much sense. But, how would being balanced with both masculine and feminine look like in a person's life?"

Malkuth smiled at Harold. "Your questions are coming from a more balanced place than from when we started our work together many days ago. Your masculine has asked the question. Now close your eyes and go inside yourself and find the answer from your feminine.

Harold closed his eyes and silently asked the question again and let go of any need to find an answer. He entered that still place that was beginning to become more familiar to him from his regular practise of being present exercise, which he did every day.

Within seconds the answer was there, and he opened his eyes and spoke.

"Being and doing is the natural flow of life. When we are present with life, present with doing, from washing the dishes or making a bed to conducting a business meeting or climbing a mountain, every action is creative, inspired, intuitive and powerful. And yet gentleness permeates our power and people feel that. An aura of receptivity and openness is created, a relaxation and safety are created, because such a balanced power has no need to prove itself, to control or to manipulate others or even oneself. Even walking from one room to another is an inspiration, an act of aliveness. You can see that in the way a person holds themselves and how they move. They seem to be thinking and feeling upward instead of downward.

"There is freshness with every action that is not coming from habit or mechanical-ness. Every action even already done a thousand times is like the first time, being brand new. Not being able to step into the same river twice, as the flow of water is not the same water that was there a minute ago, it is brand new. Likewise, each passing minute is unique and brand new with a host of brand new feelings, thoughts and physical sensations to explore in this new unfolding universe. Every day, every minute and second is brand new with every thought, feeling and action. When we are not present, life becomes boring, repetitive and mechanical. Depending on earlier life choices and decisions that we made will determine which imbalance we unconsciously fall into and lose ourselves – our masculine intellect and action, or our feminine side of being run by our feelings with little integration of the two.

"How do these show themselves in the world? The world is tense! You can see it on the faces of people as they hurry to work every morning. Tense in the rush hour traffic, busy and busier as deadlines must be reached, tasks must be achieved. It is a very simple translation of what is going on inside people. Much of the world even promotes tension in the form of excitement as seen in entertainment, horror movies, adrenalin- pumping sports and activities that give people a sense of aliveness when they are tense. Their aliveness becomes artificial and contrived.

This imbalance of the two great powers and the lack of presence, which could be described as a form of psychic sleep, is the norm in every society in the world. People run governments, corporations, education institutions and raise families in a state of sleep. People end their lives thinking that they have lived, where in fact they only experienced small fragments of life and from brief moments when life invited them back through intense events that created intense experiences. Every day offers a multitude of opportunities to wake up, when others act unkindly, mishaps occur and conflicts with neighbours or family members. Most miss the invitation and fall even more deeply into fear, unconsciousness and victimization.

"Living in presence with oneself, creates the equal balance of feminine and masculine, which in turn creates harmony, elegance, relaxation, with the potential for dynamic action when required. This is a life that is fully lived, a life living from a person's own authentic self, the true self. Such a balanced life still has the challenges of other people's unkind behaviours, mishaps and conflict with other people, but the difference is that coming from such a space of balance, these easily get resolved and each event offers the opportunity to expand consciousness even further. The results of such a balanced and conscious life will be more love, joy and inner freedom."

Harold paused and savoured the message from his own voice, then added, " These words have such wisdom, a wisdom that I normally hear from you. Now I am beginning to understand where your wisdom comes from."

"Yes, Harold, the same place that you have been speaking from."

"Now I realise why you encourage me to feel more, being so damn intellectual, to feel my feelings more and to read the tablets, not from my head, but from my heart. I notice every time I do that; this amazing feeling comes over me and then it's like someone else is reading through me and I am blown away by the wisdom that pops out of my mouth."

"It is called intuition, Harold. With feelings you start to open up the power of intuition, which includes the powers of creativity and inspiration. There is no greater power than intuition and we will talk more about that in the coming days. Humanity lost this power when it identified itself with gender and favoured the intellect over emotions and a great imbalance resulted. It is the task of every human to come back into balance and come home to their powers. Working with your feelings is the most direct way to do that. There is a great North American Indian saying that highlights this: 'The greatest journey you will ever make is from your head to your heart.' "

Chapter Nineteen
Alicia

Jonathan was lying beside the river hole where he swam each day. This was the exact spot that he had felt the prying eyes upon him for the last three days. The day before he had found the footprints of a not large person, probably a teenager, who was observing him from that location and so he had decided to prepare a surprise for whoever it was.

He had cleared some of the undergrowth so that from this position beside the river, where he was now lying, which would enable him to see the legs of a person approaching without them realizing it. But his master plan was that he had set a trap to catch the person from where they mostly hid below the river bank at a sharp curve in the river. This had been a clever place for the person to hide and observe him, without being seen, as it was directly behind a clump of undergrowth. His trap was not dangerous where the person would be injured, but just a simple snare so that when his daily observer stepped in to it, the trap would spring closed, a noose of rope wrapping itself around both feet, and the more they tried to escape, the tighter it would become. This would give him enough time to leap up and jump over the bank blocking their escape route. He silently thanked Arizona for all the traps he'd shown him.

Yes, there was a slight movement in the undergrowth. A person was approaching. He suddenly realized that he had left the revolver in its holster further along the bank where his towel was. He cursed himself for not being fully prepared. Then a pair of bare legs and then very short jean shorts, as worn by teenagers, came into view. The legs appeared to belong to a young person of about fifteen or sixteen and he moved, unaware that he himself was being watched by Jonathan. The boy moved to behind the clump of undergrowth and all was silent. The suspense was almost overwhelming for Jonathan as he eyed the clump of bush waiting for the snap of the trap.

'Snap!' The trap triggered with a sudden squeal of fright from the teenage boy. Jonathan was on his feet in a flash, sprinted to the bank and leaped over it to land facing a boy with longish hair sitting on the ground and struggling to free himself from the snare. Where Jonathan landed, the ground was uneven, and he lost his balance, falling backwards into the river. Before Jonathan could pull himself out, the boy quickly freed himself, leapt past him and sprinted away along the side of the river, then across it at a shallow part and away into the jungle.

Jonathan was on his feet and immediately gave chase. He could see his quarry was also dressed in a blue shirt with rolled-up sleeves and he could run. Jonathan prided himself on being a fast runner, but he could not gain a single yard on this boy. Over a hill, around a tree, down an animal trail and then off again into the undergrowth, the race continued. This person knew the jungle well, and after what seemed over a kilometer, Jonathan ran out of breath and stopped. Between getting his breath back, he called out, "I mean you no harm." Then the couple of words he'd learned from Arizona, "Friend. I friend."

He'd lost sight of the fleeing boy by now, but he heard him stop running. He was only about sixty yards away. He repeated his Portuguese phrase, "Friend. I friend."

Silence, but he knew the boy was no longer moving. Jonathan walked into a small clearing on a small hill, thinking that the boy could probably see him and that he wasn't armed. He sat on an old tree trunk in full view and repeated the phrase. After several minutes he heard a sound and it seemed that the boy was slowly approaching him.

There was silence again, but Jonathan knew that the boy was still slowly moving towards him, cautiously. He started singing a popular modern song, hoping to win some trust. A few more minutes passed, and he knew that the person was watching him.

After several minutes the young person, about forty yards away, still hidden by the undergrowth, spoke.

"You not harm me?" The boy called out to Jonathan in English.

"You speak English?" Then in Portuguese, "I friend." Again, in English, "I not hurt you. I want to speak with you. See, I am unarmed, and I would like to meet and talk with you. I come from Australia and I am visiting the park with my father and my name is Jonathan. I mean you no harm."

A voice from behind him suddenly spoke and, from such an unexpected location, caused him to turn around with a start. There, twenty-five yards away, stood not a young boy but a young woman, who was looking at him closely for the first possible aggressive move.

"Wow, I thought you were a boy."

"My name is Alicia. What are you doing here?"

She spoke very good English with a strong Portuguese accent. What astounded him the most was that she was probably the most beautiful woman he had ever seen in his life. The front of her hair partly covered her face in a rumpled way that made her look rather sexy. High cheek bones, full-shaped mouth, slim body with well-muscled and shapely legs. Jonathan hadn't thought much about women for a long time and the sight of her took his breath away.

"What am I doing here?" Jonathan mumbled, trying to gather himself, "Um, my father and I are researchers."

"What are you researching?" she gently and innocently asked.

"Um, rocks. Yes, that's it. We are researching rocks in this area."

"I have never heard of anyone studying rocks in this area before. What sort of rocks?"

By this time, she felt safe enough to come closer. This young man seemed safe enough, a little clumsy in his speaking abilities it seemed and possibly unsure of himself, but safe enough, she thought.

By now Jonathan was back in command of himself. "I didn't think anyone ventured this far inland to visit. Are you with a group?"

She sighed, weighing up if she could trust him enough, but having a great need to converse with someone after being out here in the jungle for so long.

"I live near here with my father and younger brother."

"I didn't know anyone was allowed to live in the park, at least that is what the tour brochures all said."

"We normally don't, but at the moment we do, but that's a long story. So, you are from Australia? I've never met anyone from Australia before."

Jonathan continued, "I've never met a woman who can run so fast, and you seem to know your way through the bush."

"My father was a tour guide a few years ago and he showed me how to move through the undergrowth, and I spend a lot of time on my own in the jungle and I love it very much."

"Aren't you afraid of wild animals and snakes and all the creepy crawlies you find here?"

"People are only afraid of what they don't understand, and I understand the jungle as my friend." She smiled for the first time and Jonathan was struck again by how beautiful she was.

Not to lose his composure again, he changed the subject. "How did you find our camp?"

"Each day is busy helping Papa build the house we are living in and I am gathering herbs and being a teacher for my brother, as he is missing out on school, us living out here. So, I get up each morning early and walk so that I have time for me. Four days ago, I woke up much earlier than usual and it being a near full moon I went for a long walk apparently in your direction. Then I heard a rifle shot and came to investigate.

I came across your camp about an hour later and saw an older man walking with walking sticks."

"Yes, that is my father and he comes from New Zealand. I live in Australia as my mother was from there, but she died six years ago and after that I moved there."

"Oh, I'm sorry, Jonathan. My mother also died from an illness less than three years ago, so I guess I know what that was like for you."

This shared experience created some understanding and trust between them. She then continued about finding Jonathan's camp.

"Then I saw you. Just looking at you gave me a sense that I wasn't the only person in the world. But I was afraid of making contact, not knowing what kind of a person you are. But I think you are not a bad person."

"Thank you. My father thinks I'm okay, so that must count for something, I guess. I can assure you, I would never harm you in any way whatsoever."

Jonathan looked at her with genuine admiration, and smiling charmingly, continued

"My god, meeting you would be the last thing I could possibly imagine, and I must say you are very attractive."

She blushed and looked, embarrassed, at the ground. Trying to correct what he thought was an insensitive remark, he again changed the subject. "Where did you learn to speak English?"

"I studied it at the university in Manaus along with Biology and many of my friends, can speak it also. Before this unfortunate thing... um, before we moved here, I would often visit my friends in Manaus, and so we only spoke English as a way to practice. I like English language. But, now, maybe it will be some time before I get to see them again. One good thing about being out here in the forest is that I get the chance to follow my research."

Suspecting that she was holding something back but respecting her right to silence on whatever it was, Jonathan asked, "So, you are a Biologist. What are you researching?"

"I study birds. I love them, they are such beautiful creatures."

Smiling at him, she said, "Your Portuguese, 'I friend' is very good, but you need to put slightly more emphasis on the first syllable. The way you said it was very cute, like a young child." And she gently laughed. It was his turn to blush and look, embarrassed, at the ground. They both caught it together and both laughed at the dance they were engaged in.

Jonathan fell in love with her in that instant.

"I should be going home by now. My father worries when I'm away from home longer than a few hours. He is afraid I'll be taken by a jaguar or a snake, but I know my way around, having spent the last four years on regular field trips and sometimes on my own. Perhaps I may visit you tomorrow and perhaps we could swim together?"

"It would be for me a big pleasure. I can prepare a nice lunch for you. What sort of food do you like?"

"I am a vegetarian. I hope that is okay?"

"Dad will like you, he's a vegetarian too. I will ask him to advise me on a tasty meal for you. But where is the house you are building with your father? Is it close to here?"

Walking away she called back, "I will tell you tomorrow. I will come about midday Will that be okay?" and at his nod she disappeared into the jungle. Jonathan breathed out a large sigh of wonderment. "My god, I just meet a dream of a beauty princess out here in the middle of nowhere. My god, she was beautiful. I wonder if she likes me a little bit?"

Alicia skipped along the path as if she was a small child again, excited and full of joy: a feeling she hadn't had since she was a small child. She had never met a young man with such kind eyes. Quite good-looking too, but that was not as important to her as the feeling she picked up in him. I feel he has a good heart, she thought. I have never met an Australian before. 'I will visit tomorrow.' She thought.

He remembered her dark complexion and exquisite features. It looked as if she had the best of two worlds: the delicate beauty of a South American Indian mixed with the beauty of Portuguese. Very shapely in build, short and slim, which is where the impression of a young boy came from. Her image tortured him on his near sleep-walking pace back to camp and a sleepless night ahead of him.

It was twenty-four hours later, and Jonathan poked his head through the entrance to his father's tent.

"Dad, I'm just going to look for Alicia."

Harold, who was busy making notes and looking over the next tablet, turned to face him, saying, "What, ah, who is Alicia?"

Jonathan feeling agitated replied, "The young woman, I met yesterday, I told you about her last night."

"You said that was a dream."

"No, I said I met this dream, this woman called Alicia. You weren't paying attention," Jonathan said irritably, rubbing the back of his neck.

"My god, you're right. Here I am trying to be present and I can't even be present with you. Tell me again."

"It probably was my fault. I did say I met a dream and it probably sounded as you heard it, because of my excitement. She was the one who has been watching me earlier in the week and so I set a trap…"

"Oh, yes, I remember now: you met this charming young woman in the middle of the jungle. That is amazing. Sorry, son, I've been so wrapped up in my notes, and wrestling with some inner issues around these stones. And that's right; she didn't turn up today like she said she would."

"Since my break-up with Jane last year I haven't been able to think of another woman until yesterday. After her not showing up today for lunch—I know she understands the jungle very well, but I'm worried that something may have happened to her. If she shows up, tell her I have gone searching around where we talked yesterday. It's about a kilometer from here, so I'll be back by six, or six thirty at the latest and will cook dinner then."

"Okay, son, but I'll do dinner tonight if you like. You go and look for her but be careful. I'm sure Ali, what's her name, oh Alicia, is alright and that there is a logical explanation as to why she didn't show up today. Just keep your wits about you, moving through the jungle, okay?"

"I'll fire two quick shots in the air if I'm in trouble. I'll be careful and plan to get back at least by 6 pm. See you."

"Okay. I am off to see Malkuth soon, so see you later this afternoon."

As Jonathan made his way across the river towards where she may by living, he began to berate himself. He must have said or done something to have put her off him. 'I'm so clumsy around women that I am attracted to, damn it, he muttered to himself.

Chapter Twenty
The center of your fear is a great power

Sitting in Malkuth's cave was much cooler than outside under the trees where they normally met. They had just finished mediating and Harold felt slightly uneasy, a feeling he was beginning to recognize, that some huge shift might happen inside of him. He'd had this feeling several times previously when starting work with Malkuth and each time his premonition had proved to be correct.

"Are you ready with the next stone, Harold?" Harold nodded.

"I wonder if I will ever understand these slabs without your help. This one reads, '**the center of your fear is a great power.**' I thought that any spiritual endeavor would be to integrate fear, which is in fact eliminating it. I know our work emphasizes not to try and get rid of fear, but the fear dissolves once we are fully present with it. Either way we are free of it, so, to see it as a benefit is confusing. Isn't that what the stone is saying that somehow fear is a blessing? But isn't fear the opposite to love?"

"Love is real. Fear is an illusion. The feelings themselves are real, but many causes of fear are illusory. How would a person feel if they were walking through the jungle feeling happy and then suddenly a venomous snake was directly in front of them?"

"They would naturally feel fear."

"Then if the person took a closer look and saw that it was just a piece of rope, what would the person feel?"

"Relief, but already there has been a release of adrenalin into the blood stream as the results of the fight / flight syndrome and so he or she would still feel shaky until the body had absorbed those chemicals of the adrenalin."

"Remember, Harold, we have had a similar conversation about this previously, so was it the rope that released the adrenalin or was it what he or she was telling themselves about the rope that they thought was a snake?"

"Yes, what they were telling themselves. So, in fact, everyone is creating their own fears based upon how they are programmed and what they are telling themselves when an outside event triggers the inside program, that in turn triggers the release of adrenalin. In that way I can see that many of my fears have an illusionary basis, if my perception about a situation is incorrect. But it still gives me no hint about this latest tablet."

"So, Harold, read the stone again from your heart."

Harold moved his attention from his head and into his feelings and then read the words again allowing the usual altered state of consciousness to take him over as if another was speaking through him and he started to speak.

" '**The center of your fear is a great power.**' The power is not in the fear but in your presence that connects with the fear. Fear is illusory. Not knowing that, when an outside potentially distressing situation presents itself, like an angry dog running towards me or a letter from my boss criticizing my work, I will in a split-second compare, then judge that I am in some physical or emotional danger. This will release the hormones of adrenalin into my system, triggering the fight/flight syndrome, which creates the feeling of fear. Next, I will resist the situation by wanting to change it because I connect the fear with the situation itself. Then I will resist my own feelings, as fear is not a comfortable emotion. Following that, will escape into my head to find a solution through analyzing. Lastly, I will assume the fear is me and lose myself in identification with the fear. Then I or distract myself by engaging in another past-time in order not to feel my fear. That can be turning on the TV, reading a book or reaching into the fridge for a beer or piece of chocolate cake to feel better. Hence, I will have created another victim circle or feel victimized by the outside situation."

Harold was quiet as he digested the words, then continued. "My god, there they are again, the five attachments, comparing, judging, resisting, analyzing and identifying! So, they are my only problem."

"Not quite, Harold. Remember, the five attachments are as innocent as the fear. If there was a problem, it is because of what?"

"Because I am unconscious of the five attachments operating in me. In fact, they are doing me. So, what you are saying, Malkuth, is that people are not damaged by their fear. People damage themselves by trying to escape what they feel, because in the escaping, the fears get suppressed. I remember reading that a while ago, and that feelings buried alive never die, but come back to haunt us later in life in the form of physical disease and psychosis."

"Yes Harold, but because everyone believes consciously or unconsciously that fear is the enemy, no one has ever gone there; none have ever truly felt their fears. People, on first hearing that, generally disagree and say that the last time, while in a very stressful situation, they were very afraid, and were feeling their fears. This is not true because what the person was feeling was not their fears, but the resistance to feeling their fears. In fact, not even this is true because what they really felt was their escape from their fears."

"It reminds me of the words of Frank Herbert, from his book, 'Dune'. I don't remember his exact words, but to paraphrase them describes this insight perfectly. I will face my fear. I will permit its passage over me and through me. And when it is here, and I resist it not, it will pass. I will look with my inner eye to see its path. Where the fear went there will be nothing. Only I will remain."

"Only you will remain," Malkuth echoed his words as a confirmation. "The only thing that holds fear in the body is our resistance. When we stop resisting the fear naturally falls away and you can see this with animals.

You yourself Harold had a situation in Vietnam when you did feel your fears, you remember? Can you talk about it? You don't have to?" He sensed Harold's discomfort.

"Yeah, it happened when we walked into an enemy ambush on a night patrol and there was absolutely no hope of survival. The VC had cover and we were caught in the open, they outnumbered us and had surprise on their side."

He paused as the pain of all those years ago began to surface and he felt those feelings, while swallowing back the anger and the tears of pain that wanted to pour out of him, and then continued, hesitantly.

"I was so afraid, and I recognize now that I was desperately trying to escape or control my feelings back then. Probably what I'm trying to do right now." As he swallowed a sob that had surfaced. He hesitantly continued. "I remember thinking that half of the squad were probably already dead, I concluded that it was only a matter of seconds I had left before I too got hit."

Harold's, memory suddenly flooded back and before he could do anything, it burst the dam of emotions of carrying that pain for so long. He started breathing deeply to assist the process. His body shuddered as huge sobs of emotions erupted from the depths of his being. Wave after wave of suppressed explosive fear swept up and over him. On and on it went, with no sign of it abating. It seemed the strongest session so far. And then as sudden as it started it completed itself and was gone. Integrated. Only he remained.

He became aware that he had laid down on his side in the fetal position. His body naturally knew what it needed in that moment of release. He opened his eyes and saw Malkuth sitting opposite smiling. He smiled back and after some minutes he slowly sat up. As he remembered the war, the horror was no longer there. For the first time he could speak about it without being upset.

"Wow, I feel amazing. When I think back to that ambush situation, minutes after the enemy opened up on us, I realized that there was no hope and would soon be dead. So, I relaxed and decided as my last action on earth I would just be with what was happening inside of me. I wanted to be fully alive as I died. Lying there on the ground returning fire as best as I could, keeping my eye on the enemy positions, I moved my attention from the outside situation to inside and felt my fears, and... I don't know what happened, but I guess it was a miracle."

My body completely relaxed, much how I am feeling now. Then the most amazing thing happened. Everything around me slowed down as if in a slow-motion film. I felt deliciously happy and loving. I could no longer fire at the enemy because no such thing existed. In the next second I discovered an old bomb crater close to me and in seemingly slow motion I rolled into it, which probably saved my life. I can still remember with such clarity as I looked up at the stars of the night sky and how deliciously happy I felt. There was no sense of time or of the horror that was being played out all around me. I know from my studies that men in battle can become euphoric as a way to suppress their feelings. The difference with me is that my body was completely relaxed, joyful and compassionate. After a time, and I don't know how long it was, I began to analyze that amazing experience. I went back into my head and everything sped up again and the fears returned. I often wondered what that was all about. It happened a month later in another dangerous situation I found myself in."

Harold looked at Malkuth. "I am also always surprised how you know these things about me."

"Clearly, in your worst moments, you connected with your fears with your whole being and in doing so, made them fully conscious. Whenever we make our fears fully conscious, they completely dissolve.

I feel you have an insight, Harold. Would you like to share it?"

"My god, yes, and what an insight! What you just said about being fully present with my fears in fact has shown me that fear is my friend. Unconscious fear is like a little death that I try to escape from. Trying to escape my fears is a mind destroyer. A tear of inspiration ran down Harold's cheek. He felt so moved that he could say nothing more.

"That is beautiful, Harold. It is so simple, not easy, but simple. I go to the center of what I feel and feel it, be with it, experience it with every cell in my body, and in that present time no illusion can exist. Only in this here and now, only I will remain."

Harold quietly continued. "Now I can start to understand the power of the stone. **'The center of your fear is a great power.'** Power is the ability and willingness to act or not to act, being and doing. The choice to feel and the decision to go to the center of one's fear enables a person to see their illusions. This is a great power, a power that most people never discover in themselves. The more they try to escape their fears the more their fears will follow them. There is no escape."

They both remained quiet as if to honor the wisdom that they had both shared. A new excitement bubbled up in Harold and new questions arose. Before he opened his mouth, Malkuth simply said, "Yes, Harold, go ahead."

"I have a question about how to stay conscious and be present right in the middle a crisis. I know you have already touched on this, but I want to go more into detail to make sure it stays with me. Can you explain that a little more?"

"Yes, of course. An outside situation happens and immediately the attention goes to it; is captured by it. That is normal. It is in this point where people lose themselves on the outside situation.

But, you can answer this question yourself, Harold. Just tune in to the stone and the answer will come. Can you do that?"

"Okay, I'll give it my best."

Tuning into his heart enabled him to connect and he spoke.

"Simple steps to learn that will be helpful.

This process can be called the 5 steps to freedom in effectively dealing with a crisis.

The five steps to freedom in effectively dealing with a crisis

1. Recognize that you are in a crisis or feel victimized by a situation.

This may seem obvious, but most people are so caught up with the outside crisis, that they fail to look inside to where the basis of the crisis is – in their fears. When people are afraid their attention is captured by the outside situation, which is why they don't access their own power. *'I'm in a crisis right now.'* Is often enough to break the outside spell.

2. Breathe

This is the time to breathe, more deeply than you would while resting normally and this enables us to come back to ourselves with awareness as well as enlivening us with its power. More importantly, the breath brings us more into the present moment, which gives us direct connection with our creativity, inspiration, and intuition.

3. Ask your self- "What am I feeling?"

What do you imagine your answer will be? – fear! Of course, your fear may have taken the form of anger, guilt or sadness and any other reactionary emotions. Behind every uncomfortable feeling there will be fear. And, there is no shame in feeling fear as everyone has it. Only true heroes feel it. The rest of us run from it, but it follows us wherever we go. There is no real escape from fear. Courage is not the absence of fear, but in acting, while afraid and in its grip. It's not important to put a label on what you feel. *'I feel terrible,'* is often enough recognition of the feelings. You don't have to linger there or get lost in analyzing, which is another escape.

4. Ask your self- "Where in my body is that feeling?"

This question enables us to come into the body that holds the fear. All emotions are held in the body as a physical stress or tension. This is the lack of ease, the dis ease, the disease that is holding the fear. To release the fear, it is important to discover what part of the body the fear is being held. The main areas most people hold it is either in the sola-plexus, the heart area, or the throat, but it can be held anywhere.

5. Be fully present with the feeling in the body

And, this is the key to emotional freedom in releasing the fear. This is putting our full attention at the point where you feel the tension the strongest in the body. This presence will not hurt you but will free you from your fear. When you put a fear or a tension under the microscope of presence it disappears into the nothing it always was. It is our consciousness that dissolves the fear. It is the great healing power we all possess that anyone can use if they have the courage to use it."

"You, Harold had already discovered this power, so it seems, in Vietnam in your most fearful moments. That is why I asked you to speak about it just now."

Harold scribbled them down on a piece of paper to commit them to memory later.

The five steps to freedom in brief:
1. **Recognize that you are in a crisis or feel victimized by a situation.**
2. **Breathe**
3. **Ask your self- "What am I feeling?"**
4. **Ask yourself- "Where in my body is that feeling?"**
5. **Be fully present with the feeling in the body.**

"Use them every chance you get, Harold. Not just for a major crisis, where it works like a miracle, but for small things as well: getting caught up in the traffic, missed an appointment, disagreement with someone you love, can't find your keys and so on. If you don't practise it on small frustrations, you will not remember to use it when the major crisis comes along, when you need it the most.

You have done great work today, Harold and I'm sure this will prepare you for the next crisis that comes your way. Let us meditate on this and let the wisdom of the stone crystallize inside of us."

Harold closed his eyes. His intuition had been right. Something huge had shifted in him and now, he told himself he could now relax. He had done his work for the day.

As he meditated he felt himself drifting into deeper consciousness. He felt deep gratitude to Malkuth and to life that this opportunity had been given to him. Drifting. Drifting deeper.

Suddenly he felt a piece of moss fall from the cave ceiling and land on his shoulder, then fall to his chest and get caught on one of his shirt buttons. He slowly opened an eye to look at it. In the semi darkness of the cave, it took a few seconds to grasp what he was seeing. Then, suddenly his mind went into disbelief when the moss moved and took the shape of a large tarantula. He jumped and in panic called out.

"Shit get it off me! Get it off me, quick!" and terror took him over. The spider was aware of his extreme fear and raised its fang and front legs in defense and at any moment threatened to spring at his throat and sink its fangs into him. Malkuth's soothing words reached him through the layers of swirling chaotic fear.

"Harold, the spider is a part of you. You are not separate from it. Only your fear and judgments are separating you both. The spider is just a part of your unconscious that is fighting with itself. Breathe and feel what you feel. Feel it."

Harold closed his eyes in the hope that by not seeing it, it might disappear. Opening his eyes, he saw that the spider was slowly and aggressively moving up towards his throat. No other moment in his life had been more terrifying than this. He was even too petrified to sweep it off him with his hand. It was now only centimeters from his throat and close to bare skin. The knowledge sped through his mind that a tarantula's bite was not fatal, but he was sure that if that happened, he would surely die of a heart attack from the shock. His feelings closed down and went numb.

Malkuth kept gently talking, as if he was calmly giving a weather report and that there was no great drama happening here at all, but respectful of Harold's process.

"Feel the fear, Harold. This is your great and noble moment. Where in your body is holding that fear?"

Knowing he had only seconds left before the creature would be on his throat, he moved his attention from the spider and to where he felt the numbness the most, which was in his abdomen. It was hard like a piece of concrete. Closing his eyes to focus more rather than to escape, he went to the centre of the energy in his abdomen like a laser beam. He felt it and allowed the fear to take him over.

Consciousness returned. The fear was diminishing, and a new confidence was growing. A joy began to enter him. He felt a oneness with what was now becoming his new friend close to his throat. He felt it stop moving. He opened his eyes and saw it through different eyes and it was no longer in a threatening posture. The creature was feeling his new energy and felt itself safe.

In that moment he realized what spiders, and this one, meant to him. The day that the tarantula crawled on him in Vietnam was the same day that his friend had been killed and two others wounded. It had been during the middle of the Communist Tet Offensive, February 1968. From that moment, every spider became an unconscious symbol for hate, pain, killing and loss. Every time he encountered a spider, it would activate this unconscious fear in him that he had programmed in himself thirty-five years previously.

Now with his inner eye he could see the path of his fear and where the fear had gone there was nothing. Only he remained. He looked with loving eyes to a creature that had helped him see the truth; and indeed, he was free.

Chapter Twenty One
Jungle crisis

Jonathan sat down on a log in frustration. He had searched for several kilometers in the direction Alicia had taken two days earlier and there was no sign of her. Besides, she might not be pleased to see him if he found her place and suddenly turned up uninvited. No, it was time to resign from finding her. A pity though, he thought.

Absentmindedly, he placed his hand down beside him on the log to help push himself up and where he placed his hand something squirmed beneath it. Quickly looking down he saw the head of a large snake a split-second before it sank its fangs into his arm just above the wrist.

"Oh shit!" he uttered as he leapt away from the log. The snake quickly disappeared behind the log and down a hole before Jonathan could properly see and identify it as a venomous variety or not. Immediately, swelling began around the two punctures in his skin.

"Oh shit, no." He breathed out and quickly thought what to do next. He tried to remind himself that there were more non-venomous snakes than poisonous ones. If it was a poisonous bite, he might have twenty minutes left and he was at least three kilometers away from camp, at least two hours' walk through thick jungle. He took off his back pack and grabbed inside it for the first aid kit and, ripping it open, he pulled out a bandage. Quickly tying it tightly above the wound as a tourniquet, he hoped that it would slow down the spread of poison. Then, swinging the pack onto his back, he slowly started walking home. Moving quickly would speed up the spread of the poison, but within minutes he felt light-headed, and sweating profusely he started experiencing breathing difficulties. It was clear that it was venomous, but not having seen it, he couldn't tell just by how much.

"One minute of not being attentive and it could cost me my life, fuck!" he mumbled to himself and felt his fear gripping at his throat. Perhaps he should fire a shot into the air, but he knew that Harold would be with Malkuth about now. Remembering that they were now working in Malkuth's cave and probably wouldn't hear it anyway made it a waste of time. "I have to slowly head for home" was his only thought.

―――

"Afternoon, Harold. Are you ready for the next stone?"

"Hello, Malkuth. I think so, yes. Yesterday was probably the most important day of all our work together so far. It made me realize just how much fear I am carrying around with me. Because I am so afraid, isn't that a disadvantage in my spiritual work? I mean, I picked up so much in Vietnam that only yesterday did I start to work with it."

"Not at all. It's not how much fear we have or don't have that determines our spirituality, but how conscious of it we are. A person with a lot of fear and aware of it is freer than a person with much less fear but not connected to it. It is not fear but consciousness that determines our spiritual state."

Harold continued, "Knowing that fear is not my enemy, but my friend as soon as I make it conscious, is perhaps the greatest revelation of my life. Something Jonathan said to me while we were still trekking our way through the jungle on our way to here, about love. He made a comment that showed me that people, especially me, don't really love those that they worry about, because we are more fearful about how we would cope if something terrible happened to them. Worry is just an unconscious fear and people call it love. That was the beginning of this revelation."

The mention of Jonathan's name caused Malkuth to suddenly raise his hand for Harold to stop talking. Looking up, he suddenly said, "Jonathan is in trouble. Quickly, think of your son."

"What's happened?"

"No time, Harold. Think of him."

Feeling the urgency in Malkuth's voice, he closed his eyes and brought the most recent memory of Jonathan into his mind.

"Now," Malkuth continued, "feel your love for him, as strongly as you can."

Trying not to let his fear get the better of him in this moment of not knowing what was wrong, Harold thought of those wonderful times he'd spent with his son and the love was there.

"Feel your fears if they are there, Harold. It is important not to deny them at this moment and as you feel them, then return to the memory of Jonathan and then feel your love for him."

Five minutes passed, and then Malkuth spoke again.

"That should give us enough time." Standing up and preparing to leave, Malkuth continued, "Jonathan should be okay. He has been bitten by a snake. It is very poisonous, but he should not die, however that will depend on decisions he is making in this moment. We do need to get to him within the next 45 minutes or there is always the possibility that it could be a different outcome. We must quickly go to him now. There is no time to lose."

Harold followed Malkuth into the second room of the cave, where Malkuth pulled out a canvas bag from beneath a rug and then looked at Harold. "How is your ankle? Can you move quickly with me or perhaps stay here?"

"If Jonathan is in trouble I'm coming with you and you can be sure I'll keep up with you."

Out of the cave and heading north they both half ran, half fast walked. Harold felt a tight feeling of fear in his abdomen and was too afraid to ask Malkuth what Jonathan's current state was, sure that Malkuth would know. He was impressed by how Malkuth could follow the lie of the land like an experienced bushman, like Arizona.

Fifteen minutes later and Malkuth turned to Harold and still walking quickly said, "Can you travel a little faster?"

"Yes," Harold lied as he felt the ever-increasing pain in his ankle.

He favored his left leg and after about another kilometer the pain in his right ankle was becoming agonizing, but no way was he going to stop. Each step sent an agonizing energy to his damaged ankle.

"How will we find him in a trackless wilderness?"

Malkuth looked briefly back at Harold and nodded his respect for the courage Harold was showing in keeping up with him on his injured ankle.

"We will find him. We are getting close."

Harold's embarrassment about asking such a stupid question and already knowing the answer was outweighed by the stabbing energy in his ankle that was now spreading to the rest of his foot and lower leg. He knew that each step was causing more damage. But there were far greater things at stake.

Ten minutes later and around a bend there was Jonathan lying on his back, unconscious. Malkuth reached him first, felt his neck for a pulse, and then removed the bandage to allow the blood to circulate into Jonathan's gorged hand. From his bag he pulled out some dried leaves, rubbed them in his hand, then put the crumbled leaves into his mouth, chewed them, and mixed them with his spittle. Then, placing his mouth next to Jonathan's arm, he spat them onto the wounds of the snake bite. Then he kneaded the leaves with his spit into the wounds vigorously, causing some blood to flow from the force of it. Next, he began to gently massage both sides of Jonathan's neck, and then other various places on Jonathan's body. Harold guessed that it was to help the flow of blood to transport faster whatever substance he had put into the wounds.

Jonathan was breathing unevenly and was very pale, but he was alive. Harold felt relieved that whatever Jonathan's chances of survival were, they were greatly increased by Malkuth's efforts and sense of presence.

After about five minutes Malkuth stopped and looked at Harold. "The danger has passed. He will live. He was very close to it and if we found him five minutes later than we did, he would surely have passed over. How is your ankle, Harold?"

"Very sore, but it seems that I am in better shape than Jonathan is. Thank you for what you did. That is the second time you have saved our lives. What do we do now?"

"In about thirty minutes, he will come around. Get him to drink this fluid." Malkuth handed him a small black bottle and some leaves, different to the ones he had used directly on the wound. "And he should eat these leaves. Half an hour after that he will be recovered enough for you both to make your way home. He should rest for the next two days and there will be no permanent effects from the bite at all. I will leave you now and we will continue tomorrow. Can you find your own way home, Harold?"

"Yes, of course and thank you again."

Twenty-five minutes later Jonathan slowly opened his eyes and the sight of his father was almost unbelievable. Feebly he spoke.

"Dad is that really you or am I having another vision like I had with mum?"

He closed his eyes again and felt totally exhausted. Harold placed his hand on Jonathan's chest and gently rubbed it. "You are going to be okay, son."

"How did you find me?" Jonathan asked weakly.

"Malkuth found you and put some herbs on your bite and you are going to be alright."

Opening his eyes again, he lifted his head to look around, "Where is he? I need to thank him."

Then his head rolled back, too heavy to hold up.

"Here, drink this." Harold placed the black bottle to Jonathan's lips and he drank.

"God that tastes awful, what is it?" Jonathan whispered.

"Malkuth said to drink it and eat these leaves and you will be fine."

Chapter Twenty Two
Being truthful to the moment

The next day Harold was seated opposite Malkuth in his cave, having discussed the previous day's adventure and getting Jonathan home safely. Jonathan was resting, having felt as though a bus had run over him, but other than that he was alright. Harold had been pleasantly surprised that despite all the pressure put on his injured ankle the previous day, today it was no worse for wear.

"I don't know where to begin to express my thanks…"

Malkuth, smiling raised his hand for Harold to stop. "The gratitude you feel for me is enough thanks. I feel it."

Both men looked at each other and the love they shared, no words could describe. Finally, the overwhelming feelings of love became too much for Harold and, embarrassed, he had to look away and change the subject.

I have a question about something we have already covered, may I?"

"Of course, dear friend."

"After our discussion on benefactors and teachers and it basically is about taking responsibility for one's own life, I am detecting that there is a part of me that wants to remain a child and not take that responsibility. Intellectually, I want to grow and be in presence. Intuitively I feel that reality just is, is true. In fact, most of my being resonates with this profound awakening. But, there is a part of me that resists this level of responsibility, something in me that feels exposed, vulnerable, scared wants to ... I'm struggling even to connect with it ... wants to ... hold on to you, wants you to be my parent and take that responsibility for me. Phew, I got it out finally. Before last night I have never seen this in me before, so, it's a great revelation. But, I am still resisting it. How can I let this one go, and assume responsibility for my own awakening?"

"You are already doing it. Remember, it is not about awakening, but to be come aware how we are not yet awake and what happens then?"

Harold nodded his understanding. "I awaken. You are right. I already feel less resistance in me towards assuming my own responsibility."

"Don't expect to be fully free of this resistance overnight. In reality it can be dropped immediately you enter the present moment. But, practically because you have lived with it for your whole life and is a carryover from our childhood, it will take a little time.

"This next stone, wow, is all I can really say about it. It took the revelation about my fear to new depths, and I could not even start to express its enormity. Normally after working with you each day, I can't wait to get back to my tent to read the next slab and to see if I could understand it. Each time, I have been able to, where the day before, I couldn't. That has been so amazing, that I can only read each stone as I come to it and none of the later ones. After my adventure with the tarantula two days ago, I didn't rush back to read the next one. I stayed with my feelings and the incredible insights I had from it and my fears about nearly losing Jonathan yesterday.

On first reading this latest stone, my first thought was that we have already done this one in the third stone of being in the present moment. Then I read it again with being more present and something opened in me and I'm not entirely sure what that is. But somehow, I feel it is connected to fear on a deeper level.

"Before reading this stone, one of my concerns about working at making fears conscious, was that there was always a good chance of the fear overwhelming a person. There are some fears that most people can manage, but there are others, those core fears, like the one with my spider and its connection to the war, others from an abusive childhood or fear connected to violence and so on. How to work with these fears when a person doesn't have a Malkuth sitting next to them loving them so much that they find the safety to go to the very heart of it that always integrates it? How can a person on learning that making a fear conscious liberates them from it, if they cannot find the courage in that moment to go there and be present with it? These were the questions that haunted me for the last two days. And I'm glad that I had this time to contemplate these questions, because only this morning, on the second reading of the tenth slab, amazingly it gave me the hint to the answers to all these questions. As I read it with my feelings the understanding came through right away and that has not happened before. The insight is so amazing that I can't seem to put it into words. It was purely intuitive and so describing is very difficult. Can you help articulate it?"

"Yes, of course. Read the stone again."

"'**Being truthful to the moment.**' So far, we have looked at how making fear fully conscious transforms the illusion of it into the only real thing that exists, which is love. Making our fears conscious is indeed a great power. But the question of how to make those core fears conscious when they are too overwhelming is answered by this stone; but I don't have the words to describe how."

"So, Harold, have you noticed that you have feelings towards feelings, or more accurately said, you have feelings against feelings? For example, when you are feeling sad, do you like that feeling?"

"No, I don't like feeling sad."

"When you are feeling irritated, jealous, bored, guilty or afraid, do you like feeling these things?"

"Not at all."

"Do you like feeling happy and loving?"

Harold nodded.

"This shows that we have been trained into believing that there are good feelings and there are bad feelings. It is the same that people believe that positive thinking is better than negative thinking. There is no such thing as a good or bad feeling or thought in the present moment reality. They just are, and so-called negative thinking is the result of not being present with our feelings. We can expand this further into suggesting that people believe there are good situations and there are bad situations. But what determines a good or bad situation, a good or bad thought, or a good or bad feeling?"

"My judgments about each of those things you mentioned. But, Malkuth, if I'm honest with myself, I still have a resistance to accepting that all situations just are. It's like saying they are okay. For example, what about war and jihad, or holy war that some religious groups practice? What about suicide bombers that blow up innocent people. Surely there can never be an acceptance of that in a conscious being?"

"Acceptance can only happen at the point of integration when we are fully in the moment with presence. Outside of that state, acceptance, non-acceptance is another perception. Also, you are asking me to agree with you and take a side. The moment we take a side we are now part of the illusion instead of being part of truth and can no longer see the world objectively." Harold was quiet as he digested these powerful thoughts and Malkuth continued.

"But in answer to jihad, an interesting practice and a powerful one that was originally designed to expand awareness of the inner battles or the inner struggle with presence. Then less conscious people took on the practice and turned it into judgements against other people they disagreed with, and the inner holy war designed to connect with and integrate inner fear and pain got transformed into external holy war against others. The perception changed reality and now you have a world in conflict with itself.

War is not caused by external disagreements, politics or misguided leadership, these are only the symptoms, but people's refusal to look inside themselves and take responsibility for their own fears and pain. If it affects us directly, all we can do is go inside and deal with our own fears.

"Yes, I can now see this, so basically, life is neutral?"

"Yes, life just is and seeing life as neutral helps us to see our attachments and especially resistance. The only thing that holds fear in our bodies is our own resistance to feeling our fears. That is why an animal is not traumatized by a near death experience of nearly being caught by predator. You see them afterwards, shaking their bodies and releasing the fear. Humans generally carry their trauma for a lifetime and never become free of it. All because of their refusal to feel their fears and resistance.

"Life just is, but people are quick to put an interpretation on experience based on their own values, beliefs and attachments, as we have previously discussed. They judge life and the things that happen to them according to their own filters, which explain why so few can see the truth of their situation. They don't see that the broken relationship could lead the person into connecting with their fears and wake up to the magnificence of themselves. People don't see that the accident was not a curse, but an opportunity of moving them to experience higher consciousness. They are too busy looking at fragments of life through the lenses of their filters and blaming it for their suffering instead of being present with their moment, which would eventually allow them to see the wholeness of life. It's like looking through a window that has water running down it from rain and believing that the distorted shapes that we see outside is the truth. Does this make sense to you, Harold?"

"Most certainly and it reminds me of a wonderful story I read a few years ago from ancient China that highlights this. Can I tell it to you?"

Malkuth nodded, smiling.

`There was an old man in a village. Even though he was very poor, kings were jealous of him because he had a beautiful white horse. A horse of such magnificent beauty, strength, and pure whiteness had never been seen before. Noblemen and kings offered fabulous prices for the horse. But the old man said, "This horse is not a horse to me. He is a friend, not a possession. How can I sell a friend?" The man was poor and there was every temptation, but he never sold the horse.*

One morning he discovered that the horse was missing. The whole village gathered. They said, "Foolish old man! We knew that someday the horse would be stolen; and you are so poor! How could you protect such a precious thing? It would have been better to sell it. You could have fetched any price you asked. Now the horse is gone and it's a great misfortune!"

The old man said, "No, wait. Simply say that the horse is not in the stable. This is a fact; everything else is a judgment. Whether it is misfortune or not, how do we know... how can we judge?" The people said, "Don't try and fool us! We may not be great philosophers, but no philosopher is needed. It's a simple fact that a treasure has been lost, and it's a misfortune."

The old man said, "I will stick to the fact that the stable is empty, and the horse is gone. I don't know anything else. I don't know whether it's a misfortune or a blessing because this is just a fragment. Who knows what is going to follow?"

The people laughed and thought the old man was mad.

After fifteen days the horse returned. He had not been stolen. He had escaped to the wilderness, and not only had he come back, he had brought a dozen wild horses with him. Again, the people gathered, and they said, "Old man, you were right, and we were wrong. It was not a misfortune, but a blessing. We are sorry that we insisted."

The old man said, "Don't be too hasty! Just say that the horse is back, and that twelve horses have come with him, but don't judge. Who knows whether it's a blessing or not? It's only a fragment. ... unless you know the whole story, how can we judge? You read the page of a book, how can you judge the whole book? You read the sentence of a page, how can you judge the whole page? You read a single word in a sentence, how can you judge the whole sentence? Life is so vast. A fragment of a sentence and you judge the whole. Don't say that this is a blessing. Nobody knows, and I am happy in my non-judgment."

This time the people could not say much; maybe the old man was again right. So, they kept silent, but inside they knew well that he was wrong. Twelve beautiful horses had come back with the white horse. A little training and they all could be sold and would fetch a fortune. The old man had a son, an only son. The young boy started to train the wild horses; a week later he fell from one of them and his legs were broken. The people gathered again, and people are people everywhere; again, they judged, as judgment comes so easily.

The old man said, "You are obsessed with values! Say only that my son has broken his legs. Who knows whether this is a misfortune or a blessing? Nobody knows. Again, a fragment and all is never given to you. Life comes in fragments, and to judge the part is to assume you know the total."

After a few weeks the country went to war with a neighboring country and all the young men of the village were forcibly taken for the military. Only the old man's son was left because he was crippled. The people gathered crying and weeping, because from every house young people were being taken away. And there was little chance of their coming back, because the country that had attacked was powerful, and the war was being lost. They would probably all die.

The whole village was weeping, and they came to the old man and they said. "You were right, old man. God knows you were right! This proved a blessing. Maybe your son is crippled, but still he is with you. Our sons are gone forever! At least he is alive. And by and by he will start walking, even if it be with a limp, but he will be okay."

The old man again said, "It is impossible to talk to you people. You go on and on – judging and judging. Only say this: that your sons have been taken away, and my son is still here. But nobody knows whether it is a blessing or a misfortune! Nobody will ever be able to know it" ;*

"Thank you, Harold, that is a great story."

"Yes, it touched me deeply when I first read it. I can see when we divide our world up into good and bad we start to live in duality and separation and this must cause a split in our psyche.

We start looking for the good and avoiding or denying what we judge as bad. And everything we avoid or deny must inevitably come back to us in one form or another."

"Indeed, Harold, and this supports the illusion of duality. Good and bad are the shadow of each side and both are coming from illusion, because there are no

---

* 1 – written by Lao Tzu

good and bad in the present moment. Here and now, just is. The moment I add anything to just is, I'm into should and should not's, I am into attachment, into values, and have separated myself from the truth of this moment, separated myself from reality.

So, Harold, coming back to the stone and that we have feelings towards feelings. How would you describe such a process?"

"I guess I would call that resistance to feeling my feelings."

"And, when you feel angry, how do you feel about your anger?"

"I feel terrible, out of control and that I must take back that control by any means."

"So, you are fighting with your feelings?"

"Yes, I'm a great fighter. But, I can see that I am in effect fighting with my feelings, which is my form of resisting feeling them."

"That perhaps is only one way we are resisting our feelings. When you feel sad, how do you deal with such a feeling, your sadness?"

"A strong resistance to feeling this way and so I immediately go to the fridge for a beer, turn on my computer, find someone to blame for why I'm feeling this way. What else do I do? Oh yes, I pick up a self improvement book and within minutes I feel better."

"So, you are escaping the feelings by distracting yourself with some other activity or a better feeling?"

"Yes, that's me alright."

"So, what resistant feelings do you have towards your fears when you are afraid, Harold? In other words, when you are afraid, how do you feel about it?"

"Two days ago, when that spider fell on me I went totally numb. After the initial wave of terror, everything closed down and I felt nothing."

"You were freezing your feelings, denying them in order not to feel them, yes?

"Oh yes. That is exactly what I did 35 years ago when I closed my feeling about my friend getting killed in Vietnam and it was the same day that a tarantula crawled on me and that spider became associated with the horror of it all. I froze a part of my consciousness; I blanked it even out of my memory in order not to feel it."

"It seems that everyone either fights, escapes or freezes themselves, when faced with a perceived life-threatening situation. This is the truth of many moments of our lives. Even a subtle, unexpected criticism from a partner or boss can set off these deep feelings of resistances in us. We feel many different emotions and feelings and we unconsciously fight with them, or escape them, or freeze our feelings toward them, cutting off from them. It is all done unconsciously, as we totally identify with them.

"So, what could be a key question that a person could ask to turn on intuition that would lead us home, the insights you had this morning?"

Picking up the stone slab, Harold read it silently, trying to read it with feeling, but nothing came.

"Maybe you are trying too hard, Harold. Perhaps relax and know that no answer needs to be found. It is the intellect that is seeking the answer, as it's trying to do the work of intuition and it never will be able to. Your intellect has already done its job, so relax and let whatever comes and who cares what that is?"

Harold looked and read the stone again without the need to know or find an answer and the understanding of the morning returned. As intuitive understanding reached his heart, tears trickled down his cheek with inspiration. The feelings of inspiration were for him the same as love and often this part of the process was joyful and almost emotionally overwhelming as he connected to his power. This was the entrance and access to all information that has ever been and ever will be. The knowledge of the universe opened to him as he spoke.

When faced with a crisis involving resistance, an additional question can be added to the 5 steps to freedom when examining what we feel. But, first I want to remind myself of the 5 steps.

The five steps to freedom:
1. **Recognize that you are in a crisis or feel victimized by a situation.**
2. **Breathe**
3. **Ask your self- "What am I feeling?"**
4. **Ask yourself-"Where in my body is that feeling?"**
5. **Be fully present with the feeling in the body.**

"The first question, **'What am I feeling?'** a second question can be added

"How do I feel about this feeling?" or **'Do I like this feeling?'** The 'NO' that comes back is the very heart of resistance. Then, be present with the fear feelings in this 'NO'. Where in my body is this 'NO'? Go to the center of this 'NO', and then expand my attention to include all of this, 'NO'. I make this resistance, this 'NO', fully conscious. I fill myself up with this 'NO'. I expand my awareness of this 'NO' by feeling my whole emotional and body energy that doesn't want to feel this feeling. I let it possess me. I am fully present with this 'NO'.

"As consciousness grows, integration happens and not only does the resistance transform into peace and balance, so does the fear triggering the resistance and the belief that generated the fear. All are integrated into the oneness of love, for love is the only thing that is real."

Again, Harold was silent and felt what he just said in every part of him. The knowledge from his intuition was being accepted by his mind and body. A transformation was slowly taking place inside him. Malkuth spoke.

"The magic of your words shows that this process works when there is no intention to make it work. When there is no aim to change, fix or transform, for such motives are born from the belief and the fears that there is something wrong with resistance. There is nothing wrong with opposing feelings, any more than there is with any other feeling. Resistance just is. We all have a committed fixer inside of us that is obsessed with self-improvement, happy endings, successful results, and that is ever in search of feeling good or better. It is part of the mental program to seek pleasure and avoid pain, the two deep hidden or unconscious motivations that run most people's lives. This is the ego that supports the belief in good and bad and keeps the two hidden motivations of pleasure and pain remaining in an unconscious state. And there is nothing wrong with our fixer. When we are present with our fixer is the same when we are present with our resistance, they dissolve into the nothing from which they came."

Harold spoke quietly, in reverence to the moment of such wisdom that was being discussed between them.

"'**Being truthful to the moment.**' When I'm resisting my feelings, this is the truth of this moment. Being present with what is actually happening brings me into the here and now and leads me home."

"Indeed, yes, but I sense you have another question."

"Yes, but it is nothing about the work, but more about my good fortune of discovering this wisdom. How is it, that I am here with you, Malkuth? Was I selected by life or by some other means, or was it an accident of fate? How has it happened?"

"You chose to be here, Harold. No one chooses us. It doesn't work like that. We choose ourselves, consciously or unconsciously, when we are ready."

"Okay! Was it because I had prepared myself with all the books and seminars I had previously done?"

"The books and seminars were actually a block in your way. You would have chosen sooner if you had not cluttered up your mind with so much spiritual knowledge. It was because of your heart and renewed choices to love and be peaceful that did it. Meditation that you regularly practiced was particularly helpful in bringing you here. Even though you had killed men in battle, lived by fear and anger much of your life, maintained strong beliefs in how life should be, lived by the 5 attachments, at some stage you made new choices to open your heart and start to feel the pain of your past and feel the love for your family. Helen, your wife was a huge influence on you in this direction."

"Yes, she made me feel safe, to feel and even cry in front of her, something I couldn't do before she came along."

"You are here because of you and your willingness to be honest with yourself, your beliefs, unconscious motives and especially your fears. Also, your willingness to know the magnificence of yourself. And I am happy that you made that choice to listen to your heart rather than your head."

Chapter Twenty Three
Alicia Returns

"Jonathan."

The sound of her voice caused him to sit bolt upright. There she was, walking towards him from the other side of the river. He leapt up, feeling light-headed from standing up so quickly, nearly caused him to faint. Standing still, gathering himself, then slowly walked down to the river's edge to meet her.

"I didn't think I'd ever see you again."

"I am sorry. I couldn't come four days ago when I said I would. My brother came down with a fever and I needed to stay and take care of him. I'm sorry for not keeping my word."

"Is he okay? We have some drugs here that might help. My father decided to bring a whole chemist shop along with him and you are welcome to any of it."

"A whole chemist shop?" She asked, surprised.

"Well maybe not." To hide his nervousness, he had attempted to make a joke. "But, I have told you a million times that I don't exaggerate."

She caught the joke and laughed. He was struck by how beautiful she was when she expressed her joy.

"I am just so happy to see you. I thought my clumsiness of our first meeting put you off me." He surprised himself with his so open disclosure about himself.

"That's what I like about you. You were so real and not trying to impress me," Alicia replied, smiling.

"Oh, I was trying to impress you, alright. I've never meet anyone like you ever before and I feel good about that."

"Do you always tell the truth about how you feel?" she asked with genuine curiosity.

"No, only if I can gain the advantage in any situation," Jonathan replied, feeling even more relaxed and finding that to be silly with her was easy – another thing he had never felt with other women before.

She laughed again at his humor.

"Is that how everyone talks in Australia?"

"I don't know, I'm too busy talking that I never hear anybody else."

She laughed again. "Well, Jonathan, I have never met anyone who is even close to being like you either."

"Oh dear, that means I must be a freak."

"No, not at all, but you don't look well. Do you have a fever as well?"

"No, I had a run-in with a snake and I am still recovering from the effects, but I'm okay now, thanks to my father and his friend, who gave me some medicine. It tasted like sewage water, but whatever it was, it worked."

"So, you have drunk sewage water. I haven't, how does it taste?" Alicia asked with a smile, taking her chance to play along with a joke of her own. Then, seeing his right arm was bandaged, her smile was replaced with a look of concern as she took it in her hands.

"I did this course on Reiki about year ago, which is a healing system using energy. Let me hold it for a few minutes and perhaps it will help."

He felt so good standing beside her and feeling her gentle touch. He was excited to see her again, and that within himself it was easy just to enjoy and be himself and let all manner of nonsense and a sense of playfulness come up in him.

"Did you see what type of snake it was?"

"No, it disappeared down a hole before I could see it, but I was very ill from the effects and I might not have survi…" he changed his sentence so as not to alarm her, "I might not have been up and about so quickly if it had not been for Dad's friend. But, I'm much better now."

After about five minutes, she placed his arm back beside him, saying, "Can you swim with your bandaged arm?" He nodded, unable to speak, moved by a feeling coming up in him that he had never quite felt before. Removing her clothes revealed a bikini beneath and she dived into the river. Jonathan was quick to follow.

Later, lying beside each other on their towels, he asked, "Why did you come each day without contacting me?"

"I wanted to, very much, but I didn't have, uhh, what is the English word for it?"

"Nerve or courage," he cut in.

"Yes, I didn't have the courage, I felt shy, yes, that's the word, shy. My father had said not to make contact with anyone in case we are…"

Jonathan finished the sentence for her. "Discovered living in the Park?"

"…Yes. I wasn't meant to tell anyone."

Looking at him she weighed up whether to tell him or not. Finally, she made up her mind.

"Yes, we live illegally here. Three months ago, my father was a wealthy businessman living beside the Unini river. Many of the locals had invested their life savings into his company. Then my father did a deal with some bad men, who I suspect were local mafia. They tricked him into signing an agreement where he later discovered he had lost everything, including all the people's money who had invested with him. The whole community was extremely angry at him, thinking that he was trying to cheat them out of their money, and for some it was their whole life's savings. They came to punish him. They burnt our house and threatened to kill us all. We had to flee for our lives into the centre of the Park, where we knew we would be safe. My father had been a tour guide in this area a few years ago, so he knew where we would be safe, where no one goes—until two rock researchers from Australia suddenly come and camp on our doorstep. We have been living here ever since. My father said that if we wait for about a year we will travel to Manaus, where he plans to start a new life and try to earn enough money to pay back all those people who lost their money. It has been very lonely here with just the three of us."

"But, you came here each day, why?"

"The sight of another human somehow reminded me that I wasn't alone in the world. I liked to look at you swimming and enjoying yourself. I'm sorry I was spying on you, but I meant no harm. I had no idea that you were starting to be aware of me, because I know the jungle very well and knew that you would not see me. My father taught me many things about the jungle. And my many research trips gave me a feeling for it, I feel here like at home."

"Meeting you was the most unexpected and delightful experience I could ever have imagined. Please tell me more about yourself," he genuinely asked with growing interest.

"No, it's your turn. Tell me about Australia and what it's like there." she smiled.

After about thirty minutes of talking about his life back home, they lapsed into a silence and lay quiet, with many unexpressed thoughts and feelings passing between them. Something beautiful was growing.

Out of the corner of her eye she discreetly observed him from beneath her arm. He was a beautiful man. She felt safe with him and was glad to have told him the truth about her family's plight. She loved the way he would chase her along the river bank and swim under the water and trip her up. His comical remarks that always put him in a bad light and yet it was not a self putdown but a self-directed humor. He was such a kid, and fun to be with. She loved that about him.

Her past experiences with men had not been extensive or anything remotely close to being exciting. Her first boy friend was a fellow-student during her studies, but she was little more than an extension of his computer.

On leaving the university and starting work as a biologist in the study of birds, she met Pedro, a fellow researcher. They often combined their field trips and very soon they found themselves in what could be called a relationship. He was gentle and kind and extremely handsome, worked out in the gym four days a week and played football every Saturday. But he was more wrapped up in his social life and his own self importance and she felt she always came second. Finally, they broke up when he met another woman and stopped calling her. That was six months ago.

The last three months of being only with her father and younger brother and helping in providing a place for them all to live comfortably in the jungle had left her little time to be with herself. Then suddenly Jonathan appeared in her life.

As she looked at him, she wanted to reach out and touch him, but her shyness stopped her. He turned and looked at her as he felt something happening in her. As she looked into his eyes, his pupils got larger and more inviting. He rolled over on to his stomach where he could see her better. His face was close to hers and she was struck by how gentle and kind it was.

He delicately brushed her hair that was covering one eye and his hand lingered a second longer than necessary and then caressed the side of her cheek. Such a simple and innocent gesture portrayed a multitude of caring.

His hand touched her shoulder and then strayed to the side of her neck that sent a thrill of excitement throughout her whole body. Wrapping his other arm around her shoulder, he softly began brushing his fingers tenderly and slowly up and down her spine. She snuggled into him, feeling safe with their closeness.

She remembered previous encounters, where they had eventually led to. It was not that she did not want to go to such a place with this wonderful Australian, but not too quickly. There was something much more here than chemistry and a desire to fulfill some physical need. There seemed like an ancient recognition of two souls that once knew each other and now reunited.

"Please just hold me," she quietly whispered.

He placed his other arm around her and she could not remember a time she felt safer. They lay together feeling each other's gentle energy, which included a galaxy of magical wonder. After a time, they heard Harold moving about the camp, having just returned from his meeting with Malkuth, and they drew apart.

They lay still holding each other's hands, neither speaking and each soaking up the feelings that were unexpressed, that spoke a multitude of something beyond understanding. The way she felt in being held by him was something she had never felt before. She was not sure she could fully trust what she might say next and it was time to call a stop. "It's getting late, and I must go home. Would you like to meet with me tomorrow?"

"You bet. I can meet you half-way if you like and walk back with you. Perhaps I can escort you home now?"

"No, I can find my own way home; besides, you need to rest up from that nasty bite. I will talk to my father about you and if it's okay with him, I would like to invite you and your father to come and visit us. We can have a meal together. But we can talk about it tomorrow, yes?"

As fast as she had arrived, she was gone. But she had left something behind, something inexplicable, indefinable, something he could only feel in his heart. Something more than beautiful had happened between them and he would never be the same person again.

Chapter Twenty Four

Thought is a good servant and a poor master

Harold made his way into the cave and found Malkuth sitting in his usual place in meditation and Harold sat opposite him, but before he could go into meditation himself, Malkuth spoke.

"Good afternoon Harold."

"Hello." Harold smiled back.

"How is Jonathan?"

"He is back to his usual cheerful self and has a new romance happening in his life, which I think is very beautiful."

"Yes, it is, and your practice of becoming present is going well?"

"Very well but I am still sometimes overwhelmed with thoughts. However, I am simply being present with them and they just disappear."

"And the next stone. How was your understanding of it?"

"Again, I understand the words but not the meaning. Yesterday's one was such a boost to my confidence, by understanding it right away, but this one has me stumped. Why don't the stones just say what they mean, instead of skirting around with double meanings or riddles? They are not at all logical in any way. Even the one that I thought I understood about the present moment still ended up meaning something quite different to how I first understood it."

"It is true, they are not logical, because logic belongs to the intellect and there is nothing intellectual about the stones. When you read them being fully present, Harold there is no skirting around. There is no riddle and they say directly what they mean. Perhaps you have been reading it from the intellect and trying to understand rather than just be present?"

"Coming from intellect, people rarely see the truth, but a reflection of their own beliefs, which they have learned or made conclusions about, often based on fear or on their value system. They see what they want to see, how they have been trained through years of living in separation from who they really are. Everything that comes into their field of experience is first passed through their filters of beliefs, knowledge, past experiences and their past conclusions of how life is. That is why you can have a 100 people seeing the same sunset and each would report a very different account. People judge others according to their own values, attachments and level of consciousness. People see things according to their own filters."

"Yes, that is true for me. I read many years ago the story of Ferdinand Magellan, the Portuguese explorer in the early sixtieth century on one of his first contacts with the indigenous people on an island in the Pacific. Communicating through an interpreter, the Islanders asked him where he'd come from and he replied from a far away land and pointing to his sailing ship in the harbor. Yet, the Islanders couldn't see it at all because it was not in their paradigm of knowledge or experience. It took many minutes before their medicine man could start to see it and many minutes more before the rest of the locals could see it also."

"An interesting story, Harold. When people are not connected with themselves because they are living from their filters, which with all incoming information has the tendency to distort or erase misunderstood parts and generalize it to understand something. Your story about Magellan highlights this. People fit things into their own level of understanding. This is not wrong, it is simply the results of society's conditioning, and eventually people will wake up when they discover being present with themselves. It is the same with you and the stones."

"Yes, that is my experience when reading the stones with presence" Harold responded. "I discovered that the same day we dug the stones out of the ground."

"Read the stone again, from that place inside you."

Focusing himself and moving into his feelings, which he noticed was becoming easier with practice, Harold read it silently and his feelings and awareness connected with the words and they surged through his body and again it was as if someone else was speaking through him.

"Thought is a good servant and a poor master. Thought is a powerful function and designed to be in the service of the true self. When the master is awake, intellect serves as a powerful and noble servant. But, because few are connected consciously to the authentic part of themselves, the master sleeps and the intellect thinks it is the true self. When it thinks it is the master, the intellect falls under the control of its own beliefs, values and attachments."

Malkuth was looking at him with his usual pose when Harold was speaking consciously, head resting on his hands as if in prayer.

"Do you understand what you just said, Harold?"

"Partly, because it is like someone else is speaking through me. What is that about?"

"In a sense it is the voice of someone that you are not yet fully familiar with."

"My true self?"

"Possibly, and with your continued practice it will become more familiar to you, and yet, you can never know it because it belongs to the realm of the unknowable."

"So, I can never know the true self through the intellect and only through intuition, then?"

"Probably quite so," Malkuth replied

"That means I only have to be present with my thoughts and see how they are running me through identification to have a distance from my values and attachments. I think I am starting to get it.

I notice, Malkuth, that you answer my questions with 'perhaps, possibly and maybe's. At first, I thought you were avoiding giving a direct answer because you weren't sure. Now I realize that it is because there are no absolutes and to make something so is like setting a principle in concrete, much like a dogma that has no room to move or develop. Am I right?"

Malkuth, smiling, answered, "Maybe, Harold, just maybe so, who knows?" and they both laughed. Malkuth continued.

"Perhaps I can expand a little on the part of the pathless path of being present. So, we are looking at two distinct paths here, the path of intellect and the pathless path of intuition and of being present. Let's look at the differences between these two paths, for they are the climax of all our work so far.

"The intellectual path is far more attractive, mainly because most people know of no other pathway home to their true self.

Secondly, all of society pushes people towards it through education, religion, science, commerce and politics. In the past, people who followed any other path were regarded as heretics and in some periods of time were severely punished, such as the Inquisition. Even today there are some religious groups that see anything that borders on the mystical as demonic. The 'correct' knowledge is among the highest values and society greatly rewards high achievers in this field. Many even believe that love, joy and freedom are found in knowledge and the intellect.

The third reason is that intellect seems safer because it can be directed and controlled, and people feel safer when things are under their control. It is logical, predictable, time-proven and trustworthy. On the other side, people feel their intuition, but they don't trust it. Because intuition cannot be directed, controlled, predicted, measured by science, is not explainable in any body of knowledge, totally lacking in rational or logical thinking, and lives in the realm of the unknowable, thus, it is looked upon with suspicion or in denial of its existence. To trust intuition is too much of a risk because logically, there is no guarantee of being able to prove it right.

People who are new to the practice of being present have some initial difficulties in walking the pathless path of intuition, because they sometimes conclude that they must choose between intellect and intuition. Such a choice would force them to step out of rationality and into the unknown of the unknowable. Intuition is not thought, has neither beliefs nor perception. To step out of thought, belief and perception is to step into the unknown. If thinking, believing and perceiving are all we have ever known, to step into 'nothingness' may be too much to ask, which is why most people prefer to stay with intellect and never practise being present, which would lead them to intuition. To practise being present, no choice between intellect and intuition need be made because intellect is a wonderful servant and therefore is a vital part of the pathless path, except that it takes second place. Often, the intellect doesn't like that.

Now, Harold, it is my turn to tell a story. There is an old Eastern fable about two beggars who lived and worked their trade beside the road leading towards a village. Beside the road was a large forest where they both found shelter each night. One of them was blind and the other had no legs. They despised each other as competitors. The blind one secretly envied the other for seeing, and spent much time bumping into trees and hurting his head. The legless beggar envied his rival for being able to walk and move about. They rarely talked to each other, except to throw insults and laugh at the difficulties of the other.

One morning they woke up and were surrounded by a forest fire. The two beggars were trapped because one could see but couldn't move fast enough before being caught by the flames. The other could move but couldn't see his way to safety. What to do, as they were not friends, but this was an emergency. The cripple said to the blind man that the only way they could escape was to work together and this could happen if the blind man put the legless one on his shoulder and he would direct the blind man to carry them both to safety. It was immediately understood as separately they would both perish. They were both intelligent people and so dropped their antagonism, became friends, and saved their lives.

How does this relate to our work here? The blind man represents the intellect, which is blind when it acts on its own. It is blind because it is controlled by its own filters of values and beliefs. It has legs and can run fast, but because it is blind it cannot see the inner sight of awareness and cannot choose a path of wisdom. It keeps banging into obstacles, attachments, stumbling, falling and hurting itself because of the numerous judgmental conclusions it makes about its perceived reality.

The legless man is the heart. It can see further and has the capacity to see into itself and awaken the truth of itself. Separately they are very limited, especially during times of crisis. Working together they can both come through the fire safely. But, interestingly, the intellect has to accept the heart is above it on its shoulders, that it occupies a higher place. The heart has no legs, only eyes and the intellect must listen to the heart and follow its directions. In guidance from the heart the intellect becomes intelligent, gentle and flexible. The person does not become an intellectual but, simply, wise.

When the two work together in this way the master's main servant comes to feed and nurture them both. And what is that master's main servant called?"

"Intuition!" Harold burst out. "Wow, what a great story. I love that story, thank you. It really shows how cooperation between doing and being, masculine and feminine is so vital in human consciousness and how the integration of the two, which includes the body, is necessary to connect with creativity, inspiration and intuition."

"Yes, intuition is like a treasure to be discovered, lying just outside our realm of consciousness and yet it is intimately connected with every aspect of our lives. Intuition is the connecting link between our spiritual true self and our physical reality. On the everyday vibration of consciousness, we experience the duality of separation, but on a more conscious level of presence there is only oneness. As we become more conscious of our three functions, intuition begins to flow, and it leads us to discover oneness and connects us with the true self.

You take over from here, Harold."

"Okay!" Taking a deep breath to help settle him.

"Many settle for just an intellectual understanding of oneness and think they are enlightened. As academic seekers of truth, people stay only in the rational mind.

Or they may settle for an emotional understanding of oneness, believing that love is the only way, and forget about everything else: a wonderful emotional high, that eventually a person must come down from to wake up. Being a whole person involves the conscious presence with all functions—physical, emotional, intellectual—and this leads to awakening of the unknowable.

There is much resistance to one of the greatest treasures in the universe. Jesus, I mean, Yeshua Ben Miram offered the practice of being present to humanity two thousand years ago and most refused it, because they didn't understand it. One or two mystics picked it up, while the rest settled for the teachings that people surrounded him with. They made the parables more important and missed the essence. People are so committed to the rational mind because what is known feels safer."

He paused to let it sink deeper into him before continuing.

"Every religion or spiritual path at its beginning was full of intuition, full of enquiry, creating a new virgin path and opening to new experiences that came from the mysteries of the unknowable. The founder was able to pass some of this inspiration to his or her followers, but they could only receive as much as they were open to, depending upon their level of awareness. As the founder passed on, the leadership was taken over by those who had received the inspiration from the founder; but not all of it, only to the degree that they were open, and so the original creativity, inspiration and intuition gradually began to be replaced with a little bit of teachings, philosophy, ritual and rules.

Then as the next generation of leaders passed and then the next, gradually there was a watering down, less of the original intuition and more of the teachings and as time passed to the present day almost the entire original inspiration was replaced by rules, ritual and intellectual dogma. Yet, the essence is still contained in every religion if people looked beyond the structure. Can you take over, Malkuth, as I think I am losing it."

"Ritual and dogma are the structure of any spiritual approach and are important as they show us the way to the essence. But many mistake them for being the essence. It can be compared to a cup of tea. The cup is the structure that holds the tea, but the tea is what gives us the inner experience of taste and therefore the essence. Religions only lose sight of the essence when the structure becomes more important than the essence. Balance is gained when we listen to intuition, while using rationality to fill in the details and create structure for understanding. Where intuition guides us, we use the rational mind of imagination to dream our desires, to pose the questions, which turns intuition on. But, there is a great difference between intuition and wishful thinking, beliefs or imagination. When the imagination or belief doesn't work, people tend to blame intuition and use it as an excuse to go back to rationality.

Because intuition is such a huge part of our lives, we all function intuitively whether we know it or not. We can understand this more clearly if we examine what rationality is. What are the components of rationality? Being a rational person, Harold, how would you describe rationality?"

"Um, let me think. From what I remember from my studies, I would say that there are three components to rationality.

1. To be able to predict and control all aspects of a person's experience.
2. To be able to measure all aspects of an experience.
3. To be able to accurately define all information associated with an experience.

I think that describes it. In fact, all these three components are needed to be fully rational, but after doing this work with you, I would say that this really only works in a laboratory and not in real life at all."

Malkuth laughed, "All very intellectual and means absolutely nothing to intuition. Anything you could add about rationality, Harold?"

"Yes, to make these three components of rationality work you need:

1. Analysis using logic and reason.
2. Space and matter are regarded as real because they can be tested in a laboratory, where everything else is regarded as superstition.
3. Time is measured linearly and therefore the past is regarded as the authority. Ah, what else, oh yes,
4. The collective unconscious is absolute and therefore controls cause, and effect and cause and effect are regarded as being real and affect all consequences. I think that just about covers it."

Malkuth smiled. "You know your rational mind very well, Harold. It seems that rationality has very definite rules, so it can function, whereas everything else is intuition. So, how rational are people, really?

For example, when we can't predict and control events, can't define or measure the outcome in advance, we don't have adequate information and so our choices and decisions are little more than a guess, shows that we are all intuitive and didn't know it.

For how many of our decisions are we able to fully predict the results? How often are we able to control events and to measure all components associated with them, or have all the information that is necessary to be rational? No-one lives their lives like this, which means that the majority of what we do is, by definition, very intuitive. Yet, we are quick to call it rationality and deny the existence of our greatest power, that of the intuitive function already in our lives.

As there is no logical measuring tool available to know what intuition is, no way to define it, so the only indication we are using it is that we are experiencing elegance, ease and grace in an environment of harmony, rather than experiencing fear and pain in a world of survival. There seems to be a sense of luck, of good fortune and ease of achievement, along with a sense of knowing, without knowing why.

Our thinking has been shaped by education systems, which are based upon the structure of logic, rationality and reason.

But with intuition, you can't put it in any reference, framework or structure. You can't describe, analyze or test it. It truly is in the realm of the unknowable and yet, intuition is everywhere."

Harold jumped in, "I read a good book on numerology a year ago and it talked about the number 2 being the intuitive number. Now that we have entered the century that starts with 2000-plus, people who are now being born will naturally be intuitive because everyone will have at least one 2 in their birth date. This confirms what you said about humanity having entered the age of presence, the age of people taking responsibility for their own spiritual lives through intuition."

"You have read many books Harold."

"Yes, too many I think. Have you read many, Malkuth?"

"I have never read a book in my life."

"What? Then how come you know so much about everything?"

"Books are the intellectual method of obtaining information. If a person only knows rationality, they will rely on this method to gain knowledge. The limitation with this method is that the knowledge they gain is probably second-hand and is based upon the perception, values and attachments of the author. Secondly, the knowledge gained is through the intellect. Knowledge can also be gained through intuition. You wish to know some spiritual truth, then let the intellect ask and allow the intuition to answer. This way the knowledge is directly from the source. And the knowledge gained speaks not only to the intellect but also to the emotions, body and subconscious, which makes it a complete knowledge. The benefit of gaining knowledge intellectually can inspire people to start working with their intuition, if the knowledge points them in that direction. The disadvantage is that knowledge gained through the intellect tends to keep a person only at this level.

We have previously discussed the purpose of the intellect, that it is not a problem-solving tool, but a question-posing tool. When the conscious question is asked by the intellect, then intuition always gives us the answer. As a question-posing tool, the intellect makes a very good servant indeed. The answer from intuition is always correct and true. If it is not, then it did not come from intuition. It is generally the first thought that comes after a question is posed, before the intellect has had time to answer its own question, which it is not designed to do. The second answer that is often logical or reasonable, is generally intellect."

"Isn't intuition a feminine quality?" Harold asked.

"It has always been regarded as a feminine quality and because male energy has dominated society for so long, it was not regarded as having any value, or looked upon as impractical, ungrounded, wishful thinking or taken seriously. Intuition isn't a feminine quality. It is an integration of both feminine and masculine qualities. But intuition is more accessible through the emotions, which is feminine and that is why it has been regarded by many as being a feminine quality.

Intellect, intuition: these are the two distinct methods that people use in their everyday lives from basic living and learning to their spirituality. They move in very different dimensions and in different directions and you can't walk both paths at the same time. However, where the pathless path of intuition includes the use of intellect as a servant, the path of intellect occasionally includes intuition as a servant. But as we have discussed, its use on the intellectual path is very minimal and for some, not at all. The more a person acts from their intellect, the less chance intuition has to operate in that person's life. That is because intuition operates in stillness and emptiness, in other words, the negative, where the intellect is very positive, busy and full. Negative in this sense is not bad, pessimistic or wrong as many people use this word. It simply means the opposite to positive and nothing more.

"Enough for today. Tomorrow, please bring this eleventh stone again and so, until then."

Chapter Twenty Five

Know the two pathways Home

They were seated in Malkuth's cave having just meditated together for about 30 minutes. "Welcome, Harold. How are you feeling, today?

"Really great, thanks. I am excited about this subject of intuition and intellect."

"Good, because I ask you to read the 11th stone again and expand on the subject from your inspiration of being present with it."

Harold replied. "I discovered only this morning that there is something else written on this stone that I didn't notice before and I suspect that is why you asked me to bring it again today. Beneath **'Thought is a good servant and a poor master'** is also written, **'know the two pathways home.'** When I became present with it, it revealed that knowledge or intuitive understanding of the 11th stone allows us the choice between two pathways. It doesn't matter which we choose so long as we are conscious of our motives and fears behind whatever choice we make. Fear will be present in both.

Now I want to steady and expand myself to fully realize what these two pathways are saying."

Harold went inside himself and connected with his feelings. Meanwhile, Malkuth took up his usual posture of resting his chin upon his two upward pointed hands. Then as Harold connected with his intuition, spoke.

"These two pathways home are two distinctly different methods of experiencing oneness. Either path will bring a person home to their true self. But because they are so different, they need to be explored to ensure the understanding behind the choice a person makes in which path to walk. One is the path of Intellect and the other, the pathless path of intuition. There are seven major areas in a person's life that can be viewed from each path and this enables a person to choose which is best suited to them. The first one:

1. Learning and knowledge. The basis of learning, whether it is through education, science, trades, or labor is designed to make life better or to improve the world. This can come from a natural desire to expand oneself in the world, or, and all too often, it is coming from a sense that there is something wrong with life. That is why science, education, medicine, psychology and many of the healing arts follow this path. All are designed to heal, fix, repair and improve a condition that is regarded as being flawed. It works with affirming positive ideas, establishing structures, systems, modalities, techniques, processes, making this approach very masculine. Historians will look back at this period and call it the age of knowledge – the age of information. The path of the intellect is just passing its climax and will eventually pass as all ages have done previously. On the path of knowledge there is much to learn in developing the intellect.

I seem to have suddenly lost my connection with myself and I'm back in my head."

"Maybe you are trying too hard, Harold. Remember, the pathless path requires no effort. Would you like me to continue for a bit?"

Harold nodded, and Malkuth carried on.

"The pathless path of intuition also seeks knowledge, but it seeks inward to the inner knowing. Intuition already has all the known and unknown knowledge contained within itself. The more borrowed external knowledge a person has, the less they will trust their inner knowing. With intuition you have nothing to learn, but to allow its presence to flow. If external knowledge is needed, by formulating and being present with the appropriate question of what is needed is enough to open intuition to provide the necessary answer."

Malkuth paused and looked at his friend.

"Perhaps you can carry on, Harold?"

"Alright, thank you.

2. Activity In the area of activity and doing, the intellect is committed to the path of motivation, achievement, of striving and stretching for success, through learning and mental understanding; the effort required of connecting with deeper levels of oneself. One has to be totally focused and do their best, to struggle with the ego and master themselves.

The path of activity is a positive approach towards success, truth, God and reality, of reaching, of enquiring and seeking towards the One. There is much to do on this path. It is the path of discipline and will-power. Many exercises, methods, techniques, systems, philosophies as well as knowledge are needed for development in preparation for meeting the achievement of one's aims, which can be enlightenment or success. It is the path of doing.

The pathless path is one of being. There is nothing to do, strive for, or achieve. On this path what a person lacks in motivation is more than made up for in inspiration. Being present with oneself leads to a naturally high self esteem because everything is a success. What is success for a person on this path? It is just being in the here and now. Nothing has to be proved or reached for. Once a person connects with intuition they have it all and above all, he/she has self trust.

Intuition is the main function of the mystic: no exercises, no methods, no techniques or technology, no doing but being. Where religion uses prayer as a way of connecting with the Divine, the practitioner of being present uses meditation or simply being still in the now as the way to connect with oneself, with one's own intuition.

The beginning of the path of activity is full of intuition, because the seeker is full of questions that turn on intuition. Thus, the information in the answers become all important and become fixed into values and beliefs and intuition fades away.

3. Values. In the area of values, the intellect wants to measure everything in order to give it meaning. On this path belief, philosophies and faith in external authorities are important. They give us value and show us the way home.

Intuition has no values because in the present moment values do not exist. In the practice of being present, values, beliefs, philosophies and faith in external authorities can be an obstacle of identification, another attachment to be controlled by, and another loss of inner freedom.

Connected to the idea of values is the concept of perfection. Anything short of perfect must be improved and worked at to reach that high state. People of this path are committed to self-improvement, fixing others, technology to make the world a better place. The concept of perfection springs from the belief that something can be imperfect. Intuition sees the world as being neither good nor bad, but simply just is. Only by putting a negative value on it can it be bad. Being present allows people to see that '**what is**' is the reality and '**what should be**' is nothing more than a learned perception outside the present moment.

4. Time. In the area of time the Intellect makes the past the authority to the future. Intellect is programmed in time and time becomes its own authority. Future considerations, expectations and planning are based upon past performances and results. For inner development, time is needed to prepare, time is the essential ingredient. You cannot be immediately enlightened. Heaven is for the future. Methods, exercise and preparation takes time, and it takes many lifetimes or through many experiences of growing to connect with Truth or Reality. Success is guaranteed, but the development is gradual.

Intuition is instant the second you come into the present moment. Intuition only knows now. Time is not needed because now is all that exists. The second you make the five attachments fully conscious by being present with them, you are here, now. You are connected. No time is needed. Success is now or never. Intuition is timeless. But this is not interesting for the intellect that requires satisfaction through the mental stimulation of time.

5. Space, Matter / Structure, Essence. The Intellect understands structure and form as the essence of anything and therefore cannot relate to anything that is nothing or empty. Therefore, it is always seeking to fill empty space. When the intellect looks at an object like a bottle it sees the shape, color and material it's made from. It doesn't see or relate to the emptiness of the space inside the bottle, unless it contains something.

The intellect is always moving, looking for ever more stimulation. All stillness and space must be filled with activity, whether it is mental, emotional or physical. Some people say that the devil works through idle hands. Others say that an empty mind is the devil's playground. Such strong words contemn emptiness and stillness from the beginning.

Intuition happens when emptiness and stillness prevail, when mental activity stops. A mystic would say: 'When you are totally empty, reality, all that is, enters.' The devil that is referred to by certain groups, a mystic considers nothing more than the ego that lives in the minds of men and woman and can only exist outside the present moment. How can ego use emptiness? Were the tyrants in history like Stalin and Hitler empty? They were very active people and were totally driven by their ego's.

What is the essence of love? Is it the structure of the relationship, such as the marriage vows, making love, saying, "I love you," building a life together and any other tangible activity or event, or is it the feelings that flow between two people that are beyond description, the essence that is beyond the structures?

You can liken the essence of life and love to the essence of a cupboard or closet. How do we identify a cupboard – by the sides, the top and bottom, the door and any draws inside, which is the structure. What of the nothingness or the space that occupies the inside of the cupboard? The structures of a cupboard are tangible, have value because you have to pay money to purchase it, but the space is free, and it is always there. If you removed the sides, the top, the bottom, the door, the cupboard would no longer be there, but the space would. The essence of a cupboard is the emptiness, the space and is always present even when the structures are taken away.

Where the intellect is positively based on the form of something, intuition is the negative side that is based on essence, that the intellect would call nothing. That is why intellectual people cannot relate to intuitive people, yet, intuitive people can relate to intellectuals.

6. Direction and purpose The Intellectual path has clear direction and purpose for life, because it is valuable. The intellect is very committed to aiming points, objectives and goals. Step by step it can be analyzed, learned, divided into easy clear directed steps because the intellect tells us that everything has a purpose. The striving of the intellect can only operate if there is a purpose. No purpose, no motivation and the intellect stops working and often depression follows. It is a path of purpose and direction to success and truth.

Intuition is pathless because it has no direction, no purpose or values, it just is. When people insist that life and love are valuable, compared to what? For a purpose to exist means that there is something even more valuable beyond itself. Without the 5 attachments there is no value, direction or purpose. Direction is going somewhere because of purpose and to get there is done in time. In Intuition there is only being here now. The purity of being alone with you and life with no direction or purpose is trusting Intuition.

7. Spirituality. The Intellectual path in spirituality is explainable, scientific, logical and structural and has the aim of spiritual survival. There are definite rules, organisation and order and with clear steps to learn and for everyone to take.

It's made understandable by giving reality/all that is, a personality and gender for people to relate to. Dogma and beliefs are aimed at explaining the Unexplainable. The mystery is explained in the words that God loves you or God is great.

It is safer by making a spiritual entity the authority that will care for your wellbeing and guide you along the perilous journey, for there are many temptations that can sway you from the path. It is more social because on this path a person is never alone. Many are walking with you and there are always markers and signposts from the millions that have walked this way before. And along the way, there is always the hand of Mohammad, Jesus, Mary or Krishna to hold. There is always a system, a method, a technique to fall back on for safety or to propel you faster along the journey.

Above all, this path guarantees success. Every person who walks this will find their God. Even though there are some groups who claim that only through their brand will Heaven be realized. Every person who walks this path with commitment will find truth, God and reality.

On the pathless path the mystic becomes a disciple to his or her own inner authority. On the pathless path you are alone with no sign posts or markers because no one has ever walked this way before. You are the path maker and not a follower. There is no hand to hold, you are alone. You can only become lonely when the intellect takes over and tries to pull you back to its path.

When you trust being present with what is in the truth of this moment you connect with who you are without explanations and even without intellectually understanding. You just know, feel and be it all.

The walkers of this path can enjoy knowledge, science and all the structures recognising their limitations, but know (not believing) that there is something else beyond all thoughts, feelings, actions, time, matter and space that cannot, nor need be explained

Intuition is mysterious, and nothing can be explained. It is negative because the only explanations that exist are those that describe what it is not.

No seeking, no striving or accomplishing, but simply opening to be receptive and allowing the universe to unfold as it will.

Because there is no seeking, no stretching to find the oneness, there are no guarantees of finding truth, god or reality. But, the second you become present, truth, god or reality finds you."

They were both silent and gently drifted into a deep meditation to crystallize the wisdom that they had both shared.

Chapter Twenty Six
Questions and answers

"Tomorrow will be our last meeting, dear friend."

A wave of fear swept over Harold, and Malkuth continued,

"It is good that you feel your feelings. We have grown close over the last two weeks. We have covered much together, and it is natural to feel closeness and some sadness at the thought of departing."

"You have become more than a teacher to me. Someone I completely trust and, umm…"

"And love?" Malkuth finished the sentence for him.

"Yes, love. I am afraid that I could never find another teacher like you, not one as good as you."

"It is true that you will never find another teacher like me, but the second part of your sentence is not true. Another teacher awaits you, one that is far more elegant, wise and knowledgeable for you than I am. Our time is nearly over. Our time has been one of preparation for your next and most important teacher, Harold.

Your next teacher waits for you in a cave similar to this one about 20 kilometers from this spot travelling due west. How is your ankle for walking that sort of distance? I notice that you haven't needed your walking sticks for a few days."

"Yes, it's okay, nearly back to normal."

"Good. There is a small mountain and a rocky formation at the base of it you need to climb a little way to find the cave. She awaits you there."

"It is a she?"

"Well, this teacher within is evolving beyond gender identification, but I refer to her as a woman because it is the gentle touch that you best need to complete this part of your journey."

"Is she attractive?" Harold asked, barely disguising his sensual interest.

"I think so, but we all have different tastes in women, so I can't say how you will find her in those respects."

"Will we share the same cave, or should I take a tent with me?"

"I understand that you both will share the same dwelling."

A shot of excitement passed through Harold at the possibility of intimacy. It was several years since being with a woman. Malkuth picked up on his thoughts.

"I don't know if intimacy will be part of your work together. It may be, and it may not be. I suggest when you arrive back in Manaus, go and stay with Arizona for a while. He is a good man. Let him introduce you to some lovely local ladies that are friends of his or family members. It would be good for you. You have been too long on your own."

"Wow, I need to think, or feel more about this, but it sounds a wonderful idea. Is it really true that our time is nearly over? I never thought that such an amazing experience would come to an end."

"There are no endings in anything that is real, Harold, remember? You are about to enter a new and very important phase of your current journey. That is the journey to presence; the journey to your essential self. I am not the one to escort you on this next step. It requires the touch and gentleness of the feminine aspect to bring you there."

"Does she have a name?"

"She has many names and I don't know which one she will use in introducing herself to you, so I cannot say. Harold, she is going to be your most important teacher of your whole life. She will take you places inside of you that I could never even come close to. It won't be easy, especially at the beginning. Expect much resistance. But the more conscious you can be the quicker, and the most amazing journey of your spiritual life will be underway. I know you will do well in your work with her."

"I will. You have prepared me extremely well and I'll be ready for her. But, I do feel sad at the thought of not working with you again. Will I ever see you again?"

"No, not in this form, but we will meet again."

"Thank you. That makes me feel better. I know I'm not meant to say something like that, I'm meant to being more conscious and should know that nothing outside of myself determines how I feel. I create my own feelings and all that."

"Harold, dear friend, there is nothing you are meant to say or not say. How you feel right now is the truth of your moment and there are no rules in the practice of presence that says you must think, feel or do anything in any certain way."

"But what about morality and kindness and honest behavior, surely these are behaviors that should be encouraged."

"Morality and rules around certain behaviors are society's invention to control what they deem as correct behavior. When we are integrated we cannot harm ourselves or anyone else, because we know there is no separation between us and another person. All is one. The concept of morality is trying to force people to be conscious, when often they are not and so the rules become the focus in what determines so-called correct behavior, and this is needed for spiritually immature people. Often, such people are afraid to think, feel and do for themselves and need external authorities to do it for them. Acting harmoniously is our natural behavior and doesn't need to be taught or enforced on people who are present with themselves."

"It is comforting to know that. What I love about being around you is that you have no judgments about me. It seems that the more values a person has, the more judgmental they have about others. There is a natural safety around people who are not judgmental."

"I think, Harold, the greatest gift you can give to another is never to try and change them and to love them for who and what they are in any given moment. Wanting to change others is a projection of one's own unwanted self."

"When I think of most religious people, my experience of them is that they are very quick to judge others, especially if others think differently to them. Anyway, when do you think would be a good time to leave to meet this next teacher?" Harold asked.

"We will meet one more time tomorrow, and then the following three days spend with Jonathan and have some fun with him and with Alicia if she is around. Jonathan is very good for her and she equally is good for him. They will experience a lot of beauty between them and, I see a lot of spiritual growth for them both by being together. They have some challenges ahead as do all alive and growing relationships.

After about three days, Jonathan can escort you and take Charlie to carry your things. This will give your ankle more time to fully recover. Once there, Jonathan will return with Charlie back to your current base camp and perhaps he would like to stay with Alicia's family."

"Yes, her father invited him to stay as long as he liked, and Jonathan said he would help him finish building their house."

Malkuth continued, "You will probably be at this place for about a week, so take enough food for two, just in case you stay there longer. I suggest not going with any weapon. There are many jaguars in the area and you may stumble upon one or two. Remember how to deal with your fear. That will be a greater protection than any firearm. This is the season of them giving birth to their young and they are particular aggressive during this time. So, do be alert and be very conscious if you should meet up with any.

When your time is over, climb up to the top of the hill and light a large fire. Then put wet grass on it and this will create smoke. Jonathan will see it and will then know to come for you. It would be good for him to bring the shotgun. Not to shoot anything, but a shot over their head will send any jaguar off. He does not have your emotional skills at this stage. But one day he will, and he will at an earlier age than you. He is a very bright young man."

"I know and more sensitive as well. Will this woman be there when I arrive?"

"Probably, but she may not be. You need to be able to read the twelfth stone first, Harold. If she is not there when you arrive, only when you have truly committed yourself to intuition will you be able to read the twelfth stone, and only then will she arrive. So, over these coming three days, take a rest from all your studies. Swim and have fun. That is what you need right now instead of serious study.

Do you have any questions, Harold?"

"Yes, I do, actually. My first question concerning learning and knowledge is, from what we said yesterday, does it mean than many of the healing arts in the human potential movement and many spiritual approaches are in fact the path of the intellect?"

"Almost all spiritual approaches and human potential methods had their beginnings completely in intuition. Their founders were walking the pathless path, because there were no sign posts and they had no other means available other than their intuition. Then many of them began to organize their methods into a teaching form and gave it structure. It still remained intuitive with the intellect and form as useful servants. Then more and more joined and learned it as a technique with aims for self-improvement in the future. Here is when the path was changed, and the technique became the focus instead of consciousness and intuition became the servant to the technique. Then with some groups as more time passed, concepts of truth became more important than realness, knowledge became more important than awareness, the end results of feeling good became more important than the process of being here now with what is. Where intellect is often more interested in correctness, intuition is only interested with what is real."

"You often use the word awareness of something, but for many people they take that as knowing about something, so what is the difference between awareness and knowing about, if in fact there is one?"

"A good question, Harold! Knowing about something is an intellectual knowing. An awareness of something involves intellect, emotions, physical and intuition. It's like standing beside the ocean or a lake and a person can know all about oceans and lakes, what the water is made from, the rocks plants and fish. The person can be an expert on lakes. Awareness is like stepping into the water and being fully involved with all one's senses, feelings, thoughts as well as intuitive connection. With awareness, there is beyond the knowing and fully intuitively experiencing."

"Thank you, yes that explains it well.

In the area of activity, doing, the intellect is committed to the path of motivation and achievement; does this mean that a person walking the path of intuition would lose all interest in all forms of activity and simply sit around contemplating their navels?"

Smiling at Harold irony, "No, not at all. The path of intuition is full of creativity and inspiration, with no aiming point or seeking results and yet, it can still be full of activity. Such a person would probably still practice yoga, physical exercise and even techniques, but their motivation would be quite different. An intellectual motivation is seeking some purpose beyond itself. The person on the intuitive path could be doing the same activity, but with inspiration to be here now. So, the real difference is not one of activity itself, but the motivation behind the activity is what spells the difference between the two paths."

"The next point about values I found interesting, but can a person really live without values?"

"The path of intuition isn't living without values but seeing how our values control us. At this stage of evolution, it is not possible or wise to attempt to live without values. Remember, it is not about getting rid of attachments, which values come from, but to see and feel how a person is trying to be someone they are not, through the two extremes of self-rejection or self-importance. All values and attachments are innocent, they just are. As a person sees and feels them, of course such things fall out of a person's life and they come back to just is."

"I understand that in the present moment everything just is and the second you add an attachment to reality it changes into 'what should be.' I remember I attended this breathing workshop and the seminar leader was saying similar things that everything just is. But I kept thinking at the time that it sounds ungrounded and flaky and seems a cop-out or a denial of the real problems in the world today and there are many problems. With global warming, pollution, and there is a huge disproportionate distribution of wealth in the world. In fact,

5% of the population own 95% of the world's known resources, which means that 95% of the population own the remaining 5%. There are at least 8 countries where its leaders run things like a mafia family, fighting to hold on to power and oppressively controlling its people, rather than being a responsible government for the people. There are religions that openly discriminate against woman. Crime continues to soar, war is raging in several countries and I could go on. I mean, the world is a mess with a million problems. I know we have had this conversation a number of times already. Help me to understand reality just is."

"Yes, you are right, Harold, there does seem to be a million problems, which means you need a million solutions. But, what you described is not the problem but the symptoms of one problem. There are not a million problems, there is only one and that is the world has not woken up to its own magnificence and power. It is still trying to use the intellectual fix and as we have discussed, the intellect is not a problem-solving tool. This means there is only one solution and that is that the world needs to wake up to its intuitive, inspirational and creative powers, which can only happen in us when we are in the free non-fear state, which is being present. Until humanity wakes up it will continue to try and improve the world using a totally inadequate tool. That is why using the intellectual method, as the world advances in one area it recedes in another and all the attempts to improve the world will ultimately fail. The symptoms that you mentioned happen because people live in unconscious fear and are obsessed with values, attachments and beliefs, which are the products of a misuse of the intellect. Does it make sense to try and fix symptoms, using a tool that created them in the first place? As people wake to their own powers, these symptoms will disappear.

If you look at your own life, Harold and the areas where you have woken up, are the symptoms of unhappiness surrounding those issues back then still with you today?"

"No, indeed not and that makes total sense, thank you, I understand it now. So, as I understand it, there is no aiming point, no purpose to anything, except to be here now, yes?"

"No, Harold, making the here and now into a goal is *denying the truth of this moment, which may be that a person is* afraid of going to the dentist."

"Ah, yes and simply be with the truth of this moment, whereas how I was saying it was seeking the ideal present moment and not being real with my current present moment. I've got it!"

"Harold, it is normal to have doubts and even resistance to reality being just is, at this stage of your journey. But, these doubts are born when we try to make just is into another concept, another philosophy to live by and so are back into the intellect of values, rules and beliefs. Relax and be with your feelings about your doubts. They will soon pass."

"I have one last question which is also bothering me. "I believe in past lives, but if now is all there is, how does past lives, karma and the law of cause and effect fit in to presence?"

"There is no such thing as past lives and for those who believe in it they will probably create parallel lives.

Everything is happening now and the reason you are only experiencing this life is because you have chosen to be present with it. The rest are all happening right now, because now is all there is. On the other side of this life it is believed by some people as an extension of a person's consciousness, which includes all the person's beliefs and being creative beings, could possibly create whatever is in their consciousness. Karma means action and reaction and, like cause and effect can only exist when people are not present with this life and are living outside the present moment, which is where people generally live. If there is only now, how can there be a cause and then an effect to follow? Yet, people experience this because they live in linear time."

"What do you believe about past lives and karma, Malkuth?"

"I don't hold to any belief. Each person must decide for themselves, but, enough for today and tomorrow we will talk some more."

Chapter Twenty Seven
A Chapter Closes

The following day was sunny with a hint of optimism in the air. Knowing he was going to his last meeting with Malkuth, Harold was filled with a mixture of feelings. Sadness, a hint of fear and excited by a sense that something brand new was waiting for him, behind some corner, a new understanding, a new level of inner greatness seemed to be approaching him. So much had happened during these last two weeks! It felt like his whole life had changed totally, never dreaming for a second that such an outcome, when all those months ago a treasure map of the greatest possible measure fell into his hands. He smiled to himself, seeing how attached to values he still was and gave himself permission to be at that place. 'How comfortable and stress-free it is to be real,' he thought to himself.

Later that day, sitting before his friend, Harold's smile revealed a galaxy of emotions. Malkuth smiled back with a sense of knowing.

"How are you feeling?" Malkuth asked

"I have never quite felt like this in my whole life and it would probably take the rest of my life to explain or even consciously feel all that I am feeling."

"It is good that you are feeling, Harold. But, I sense some more questions in you about what we covered yesterday."

"Yes, you sense me well.

I understand the basic concept of structure and essence, but something is missing for me and I don't know what that is." "Harold, dear friend, your intuition is sharp, but so is your intellect. When trying to understand a concept, where is a person coming from?"

"Intellect!"

"Yes, and when we understand that there is nothing that needs to be understood, and then understanding comes, because intuition was given the chance to be here. Intellect wants to label things to understand it, things like reality and God for example. Intellect labels the unknowable, the unlabeled to find meaning. In intuition; in the present moment there is no meaning. Intellect even wants to label the word essence. Yet, even essence itself does not exist in an intellectual reality, but people try to understand the pathless path by giving what is nothing the description of essence. Essence is nothing and everything. When people are confused by this last sentence it means they are in their intellect and for intuition, it is normal, natural and clearly known."

"So, would it be true that creativity, inspiration and intuition are connected to real love, joy, and expanded inner freedom, that fearless state, the state of bliss that many spiritual books write about, and intellect is the striving part of us that wants to realize all that intuition already is?"

"That could be one way of looking at it. This fearless, bliss or expanded state of just is, is the intellect giving it a value and then through identification, loses it."

Nodding his understanding, Harold asked, "Being achievement orientated all my life, the points on motivation and inspiration were particularly interesting to me. If I walk the pathless path of intuition and I lose my motivation because there is no purpose to anything beyond itself, am I guaranteed that inspiration will take the place of motivation?"

"No! On the pathless path there are no guarantees for anything. Inspiration is a here and now experience when I step through my fear of having no motivation. You can create motivation because it is intellectual while using the emotional center, but you cannot create inspiration any more than you can create intuition. There is no control over inspiration. There is no directing it. It is the result of being present. When you are fully present, then inspiration expresses itself through you."

"Okay, that makes sense, thank you!

Yesterday it was said that the intellectual path in spirituality has definite rules, organisation and order and with clear steps to learn and for everyone to take. But, does not the path of intuition also have steps towards understanding, like for example the twelve stones set in a precise order as stepping stones, as you like, towards oneness and understanding?"

Again, Malkuth smiled at Harold's highly intelligent questioning.

"The twelve stones are not small steps towards understanding, but only as a preparation to step from the intellectual path. On the pathless path of intuition, there are no small steps but a quantum leap into the unknown. Just one huge step into the unexplainable, the unknowable is taken.

The rational mind cannot explain or welcome this and desperately tries to get back to the intellect and explainable logic. Yet, intuition doesn't need logic or reason, but relies on itself. It requires an adventurous mind, that can let go of all steps and is ready to jump into the totally unknown, one that is courageous enough to leap into the unknowable, the abyss, for it is bottomless, empty, an absolute nothingness for your mind. The intellect is afraid of this nothingness, believing that it too would become nothing and cease to exist if it ventured there. In the present moment no such fear can exist, because it knows (not believes) that reality can only exist because of us, and without us, there would be no existence.

That is why so few walk this path, not because they lack courage, but because they did not know of its existence to come home by. Intellect does not have the capacity to know anything outside itself. That is why the intellectual path views intuition with suspicion and the same reason why some religions look upon mysticism as being associated with the occult and black magic. The occult and black magic although often using intuition, is actually on the path of the intellect because it has definite aims and are obsessed with power rituals and knowledge, which are often based on fear."

Harold burst out with, "Good lord that means that much of the intellectual path is based on fear, yes?"

"It is not so much that the intellectual path is based on fear, but the misuse of the intellect through the five attachments do create a lot of fear. And for that reason, yes, there is a lot of fear on the intellectual path. This can be clearly seen in many religions that were originally intuitive based, then changed to the intellectual path when the fear of punishment type dogma, such as heaven and hell and ritual became more important than consciousness.

Mysticism is only interested in intuition and sees all the effort the intellectual path takes is largely wasted, that the hard work of learning, processing, healing and finding truth is attained in the present moment effortlessly when you make the five attachments and fears conscious, when you connect with intuition."

"Yes, I see! What would happen if everyone in the world switched from the intellectual path to the no path of being present?" Harold asked.

"You tell me, Harold," Malkuth replied.

"Well, I guess there would be utopia, heaven on earth, with no wars, or crime or disease. That love, joy and freedom would be the norm. But, I can't imagine that ever happening considering that humanity is still committed to survival, power, and control."

"Well, Harold, if you imagine such an event, with your newly-found powers, you may help humanity keep that reality."

"Oh, shit, yes, you are right. Perhaps it would be wiser of me to look for the very best, the very highest in people. And to be ready and fully available to be an inspiration to those who can't see their own magnificence, to be there for those who are still controlled by their attachments, fears and limitations. And it's okay for people to be in that place, because that is how it is and that is reality. But, most of all, I need to apply what I just said to myself. I need to be there for me."

"Harold, you really are complete with me and ready for your next teacher. Please tell me more of the insight you are having right now about the evolution of human consciousness."

"Thank you, yes. More people are seeing the limitations of the intellect, seeing how it is always reliant on an outside source to follow, which can be dis-empowering. How on the mental level, they have to rely on other people's knowledge and motivation, because knowledge and *'improving'* oneself to be a *'better'* person is very important on this path.

On the emotional level they see the limitation of remaining in a subservient state to some higher and outside authority and relying on it for guidance of how to live, love and be happy.

On the physical level they see the limitations in so much to do, to prepare for, to exercise to be worthy enough, to be disciplined or determined enough to keep going.

More and more people are waking up to the glory of themselves and discovering that after stepping through their fears of the unknown, **Heaven is now**. People are starting to experience the more direct path; nothing to believe in, no conditions, no restrictions, no striving, no techniques, just total freedom in the essence of the NOW. In the now our true nature begins to manifest the purity of love, joy and freedom. If there is a waiting, it is the time it takes to enter the present moment, which can take a while for those new to the non-path, because they are so used to walking on the intellectual path. As more and more people start walking the pathless path of intuition, they will make it easier for others to be inspired to find themselves and their own unique path. Eventually the whole human race will wake up.

Phew, that is some insight."

Harold was silent for a moment. Malkuth remained quiet and held the space for his friend, sensing a new question coming through.

"Malkuth, what are some of the pitfalls for those new to the path of intuition, a person like myself could meet?"

"One of the first things that most new comers to living in presence experience is a deep sadness, a grieving of the old ways; the old self, the ego. As limiting as the path of intellect is the one who practices being present still feels a sense of loss. It's like losing an old and trusted friend, which the old self was. It protected us from possible hurt, gave us comfort in the belief that we would be looked after and a way to deny our pain by thinking of roses."

Malkuth paused and mischievously winked at Harold, who returned a knowing smile.

"This soon passes as the person becomes present with these feelings.

Another obstacle to experience is that there is nothing to strive for anymore, many new to this non-path can feel a sense of loss for excitement, for the thrill of achievement. This can cause some practitioners to return to the more familiar path of the intellect. But, with regular practice of being present, every moment becomes an achievement in itself. Every moment becomes an exciting adventure because each new moment has never happened before, and so these feelings of loss quickly pass.

As we start to wake up is like switching on a light in a totally darkened room. Mystics have often told us that we are surrounded with all manner of things we can't see unless we look. Then we can include them into our possible knowable experience. If we allow it to exist, it will. Like a fish that is unconscious of the water surrounding it, so are most humans unaware that intuition surrounds them. Rational thinking is the servant to presence; it is the smaller picture in the larger picture of intuition. No matter how far a person goes with rational thinking he or she will sooner or later come to a boundary where they can go no further. On the other side of that boundary, and surrounding rational thinking, is total expansion of intuition.

It is the same with the manifestation of the physical universe. On the other side of our illusion of matter, lies the realm of intuition, surrounding and including physicality. The physical plain appears to be all there is and appears so real and logical, something we can touch, weigh and measure. Science and some religions have become stuck here because of their over-reliance on reason and meaning. The physical plain is nothing more than a reflection of the spiritual intuitive plain, like the sparkle of sunlight on a lake. When we approach science or spirituality in logical and absolute ways we become trapped in the illusions of structure and physicality. The form becomes more important than the essence. Yet, Society has a lot invested in rationality, like you said, Harold, wealth, power, control and this keeps them from experiencing intuition, from the greatest treasure the world has ever known.

"You would like to add something, Harold?"

"Yes, thank you. I am reminded of the words of the master Christian in St. Luke, chapter 17, when he said, 'the kingdom of God is within you.' I wonder how the whole Christian world missed this.

Also, as I listen to you I am reminded that in the Old Testament, from which most of Western society's original values came from, the mythical story of the Garden of Eden when God warned humankind not to eat from the tree of knowledge. This may be a play on words, or a misinterpretation, but perhaps not. Also, there is a well-known philosophy that describes humans in this way: 'I think; therefore, I am,' which is putting all the credibility for existing on the intellect, which is justifying its continued use."

"Perhaps so, Harold."

"One last question, Malkuth, I want to walk the pathless path of intuition, but I am so intellectual, so full of fear, lacking trust in myself that I am afraid I will never be able to do it. Can you offer me some last-minute advice?"

"By seeing and feeling and being present with how you are not doing it. That is all. Making your attachments more conscious is enough. Everyone has had a lifetime of mental programs, experiences that tells them that the intellectual path is the safest and the most real. So, rationality is really all they know. Then suddenly they discover something entirely new and want to walk it, but are so committed to their old values, attachments and rationality that it seems impossible.

It is very possible, once we decide to commit to practicing being present every day and seeing how we can't walk this new way, how we are stopping ourselves. Be present with these and suddenly we discover that we are walking the path of intuition.

And this is it my dear friend. Here my guidance and companionship in your path ends. I feel what we have done during this time will serve you in the coming days, where your level of presence will be greatly needed."

They were both silent in awe of what had passed between them. Both were looking at each other as brothers on a similar path, and then Harold looked down in a mixture of embarrassment and in respect for the feelings of a sacred awe. Suddenly, without apparent reason, Malkuth began laughing loudly. Harold looked up in surprise with a slight irritation at such a deep and spiritual moment being interrupted in this way.

"What's so funny?" he asked.

"I apologize to you, Harold, but whenever I see someone taking something so seriously, it touches a funny spot in me. I know this work we have done together has been very important to you."

"You can bet on that. Those twelve tablets have changed my life. They are sacred to me."

"Can I recommend that to look carefully at what you just said, that they are sacred to you?"

"Oh shit, yes, I have made them into just another value and have already become very attached to them and what they mean."

"That is what happens to most people when they first start walking this pathless path. They are constantly looking to make something into a value in order to give it meaning and understanding. It is the act of the intellect. I am happy that you can see that. Anything that a person makes sacred will become their prison. Everything that a person forms into an attachment to will eventually leave them, people, possessions, concepts, they will all go. Nothing is sacred, everything just is.

Chapter Twenty Eight

The secret of the twelfth Stone

Harold followed the track to Malkuth's cave knowing that after yesterday's final meeting he would not be there.

Remembering those final highly emotional moments of standing together and looking deeply into each other's eyes, and Harold, knowing that this was the very last time he would ever see his most trusted and beloved friend. It had become too much, and he had broken down and wept openly. Then Malkuth had wrapped his strong arms around him and his whole body shook as another wave of deep sobbing passed through him. Never had he grown so close to another person in such a short space of time. Not even with his comrades that he had shared life and death experiences with, back in Vietnam, that he was sure could never be equaled could come close to what he was feeling in that moment.

Suddenly in Malkuth's embrace Harold had felt the love of his father coming through. His father had departed this life 20 years earlier and even though he knew a deep love was shared between them, they were never able to show it to each other throughout their lifetime. Right there in that moment, Harold was a small child again and being held by his father who was showing his love. After the next wave of sobbing that lasted longer than the earlier waves, a quiet peace had descended upon him and permeated throughout his body and he suddenly knew that he had finally made peace with his father. An important completion in this final good-bye through Malkuth to the man who had shared the most important part of his early life with, that had not been easy, often not joyful and large fragments of it in conflict. Still in Malkuth's arms, he had opened his eyes, looked up and slightly nodded his recognition to what was happening, and a smile of thanks and love went to where it needed to go.

Then stepping back and looking at Malkuth, he noticed that the tears in his eyes had prevented him from seeing his friend clearly. He remembered wiping his eyes to see more directly, but somehow Malkuth's image remained unclear and vague, which he attributed to the poor light in the cave and the tears in his eyes.

He remembered what happened next with a little confusion and the final words from his friend.

"Sit dear friend. Meditate on the joy of our time together and know that the signature of my touch will always be in you."

Harold had sat, closed his eyes and had drifted into a peaceful sleep, which he felt was long with many vivid and joyful dreams of being with Malkuth in the last two weeks.

He had woken with a sudden start and glanced down at his watch, which showed the time of less than ten minutes had passed from previously looking at it, just before standing together and embracing for the final time. The thought that this was impossible passed through his mind, but quickly left him, as he realized that Malkuth was gone. The cave was empty. He could feel no presence of him, which only now he realized that he had always felt very strongly, whenever they were together.

He stood there remembering the previous day's events and a tinge of sadness touched his heart as he knew an important chapter of his life was over and with a little excitement that another was about to begin.

He walked on and passed the clearing where they had first meditated together, and the carpets were gone, but to his surprise the grass and small plants had not been disturbed from having a carpet on top of them for over two weeks. Not the slightest discoloration of the plants that had been covered was evident. It was as if the carpets had never been there. How could that possibly be? Only where he usually sat was the grass flattened. Where Malkuth usually sat, there was no disturbance at all. Suddenly his thoughts about Malkuth's humanness or even his existence were coming into question.

Arriving at the cave he went inside and switch on his flashlight. There was absolutely no evidence of anyone ever having been there at all except for a small path where he usually walked but no other footprints anywhere else. The stakes driven into the walls that held the herbs were not there, nor any markings of stakes ever having been there. No fireplace, not even any ash that should have been present after weeks of cooking. This was not possible, he thought to himself. He entered the second cavern that was witness to his most life-changing experiences and again there was no evidence of anyone having been there, except his own footprints in the grey dust. Only where he usually sat was an imprint into the soft soil. Not even any signs that a carpet had been laying on the floor of the cave for that period. Perhaps he dreamt it all. Maybe he was hallucinating. Perhaps he was drugged and believed it all happened. He became filled with doubts and yet, what he had experienced over the last 15 days was the most real experiences of his whole life. He was glad that Jonathan, who was too busy with Alicia, did not accompany him to the cave. He was sure that any comments from Jonathan would have shed too many doubts on an ego already bursting to know the truth of this more than strange situation.

He thought back to the night the bandits had attacked them and a conversation with Jonathan the following day, where his son admitted that he didn't see Malkuth saving them. They had both attributed this to the concussion Jonathan had received from the blow to his head by the bandit. Harold further remembered that not even Arizona had seen him either, having been knocked unconscious. That in fact, apart from the bandits, only he had any physical contact with Malkuth. Were the bandits real, he thought to himself? He would discuss that event when he saw Arizona in the coming weeks.

He left, not understanding and knowing that he didn't have to understand it or try to figure it out. Never in his life before, would he have not tried to discover this most peculiar event. He decided to put this into the realm of the unknowable. It wasn't about denying his natural curiosity; he simply did not need to go down the track of analysis to understand. He decided to say nothing to anyone about this more than startling evidence of a seemingly non-existent Malkuth.

He would follow Malkuth's suggestions and travel due East to meet his next teacher in the next two days. Somehow the twelfth stone felt like it was the most important of them all. He was determined to discover the wisdom within it. The understanding had not come through on his reading of it that morning, but he was confident that it would in time.

The next three days with Jonathan and for some periods with Alicia were totally enjoyable. Before doing things, he noticed he would decide just to have fun with whatever it was, making him more playful and humorous, and the camp echoed with much laughter and merriment.

He was glad that it looked like Jonathan had found the woman of his life. They looked good together and so much in love. He liked Alicia very much also and was more than happy to welcome her to the family.

Three days later, they left the campsite before 7 am for his final meeting with some mysterious woman, which he suspected would change his life forever. He knew that the next time he saw this camp he would be a man looking through very different eyes.

Half-way through the journey Charlie became unusually jittery and afraid.

Jonathan whispered, "I think we are being followed by a jaguar, Dad and I think it is quite close, maybe 50 meters behind us."

"I feel it also."

Jonathan tried to soothe Charlie by stroking his neck and quietly speaking to the stricken animal.

"Let me go back and fire a shot over its head to scare it off," Jonathan suggested.

"No, you go on with Charlie, I'll take care of this."

Jonathan, assuming he had his revolver tucked in his back pack, said, "A shot gun is better, Dad if it decides to charge. A revolver won't help much."

Taking it as not to alarm Jonathan, he waited until they had moved on and was out of sight. Holding the weapon, he could feel the sole intention of what this instrument represented; death. Placing it against a tree and taking off his back pack, he stood there for a minute collecting himself. Taking a few deep breaths, he felt his fear. Breathing the fear into him until he was fully conscious of it, he carefully and slowly began to walk through the dense undergrowth in the direction of what he felt was a hungry and large spotted cat. He couldn't see it but was sure that it could see him. He paused again as another wave of fear came up. He detected an ego that urged him to go back and retrieve the shotgun, just in case. He breathed that in and the fear associated with it, and it integrated. He moved on towards where he suspected the animal was.

Slowly, ever so slowly moving and he knew the animal was close. With all his senses fully alert, he picked up the animals' scent. It was not moving, perhaps crouched down in a prepared attacking posture. Knowing the situation, he was in should have shocked even the most courageous of the brave or the most stupid, but somehow, he knew he was safe and he didn't know why. Staying conscious of his feelings somehow was his greatest protection from any attack. Knowing that the jaguar was not a separate dangerous beast, but a reflection of his own subconscious mind that was trying to conflict with itself, he kept slowly moving towards what he knew to be a part of himself. Sweat trickled into his eyes caused by a mixture of the heat of the day and conscious fear. Being so connected with his fear seemed to give him enormous courage and power. A thought flashed through his mind. This was how Malkuth must have felt when he stepped into the camp with the bandits over two weeks earlier, if in fact it had happened.

Soon the fear reduced itself to a slight tinge of nervousness and excitement in the pit of his stomach, reminding himself not to try and get rid or control it. As quickly as it came, it transformed itself into a powerful feeling of compassion for the animal close by. Slowly moving, totally conscious of his whole being, where he gently placed his next step, slowly moving, feeling his power, feeling his love when suddenly there was a loud snarl and growl, almost right next to him, which startled him and the quick movement and blur of a large spotted animal, bounding away through the undergrowth and then was gone. The sudden movement had startled a shock of fear through him, but as fast as it came with no resistance, it passed through him and left much like the departing cat. He took a large breath and smiling to himself realizing that he had mastered his fear. What a freedom. To live a fearless life by not trying to escape his feelings was probably the greatest wisdom in the world, and it seemed that he possibly had it.

Making his way back along the track and picking up the shotgun on the way, he caught up with Jonathan and Charlie. Charlie was calm, and Jonathan looked at him strangely, not saying a word, but had the hint of a knowing smile.

The rest of the trip was uneventful and by late on the second day they had arrived at the base of the hills that was very rocky. It only took half an hour to find the cave entrance and he was disappointed that no one was there. They camped up for the night and the next morning Jonathan and Charlie departed early. Within minutes of their departure, Harold was struck at how alone he felt, and it soon changed to feelings of loneliness. He returned to his tent and lay down and went into a process around his feelings. 15 minutes later he emerged and felt empowered again. Having experienced many integrations over the last two weeks he was always taken by surprise with each one. Smiling to himself his knowing that every integration is the formation of something that had never happened to him ever before. He was creating a new path of presence inside himself with every session of being present with whatever he felt.

It was the third day and still no sign of his teacher. His doubts about the reality of the last two or three weeks kept nagging at him and by paying attention to the accompanying feelings they would soon pass. His frustration of not being able to read the twelfth stone was becoming a serious problem for him. The previous days he had tried to read this last tablet many times, but he could not make any sense of it. He had even read all the others that he'd brought with him and could do so with no trouble, but this last one it was not possible. He had mediated for hours hoping that it would prepare him enough to be able to read it. He had tried relaxing and not trying, focusing and everything he knew, but still nothing worked.

He opened his eyes and looked around in the semi darkness of the empty cave. His expectancy of sharing it with feminine company had led him into disappointment of her not showing up. The plans he had in cooking for her, fussing over her and perhaps even making love had been part of his dream that now seemed like it was not going to happen.

He decided to be present with his disappointment and the fear of perhaps never meeting a woman and experiencing intimacy ever again. He had mastered his fear of spiders and jaguars and thought fondly of his new tarantula friend he'd called Henry who lived at the entrance of this cave. Then back to his feelings of disappointment.

He closed his eyes. He asked himself the key question to connect with his fears. 'What is the worst thing that could happen to me in this situation?' As the feelings came up, they overwhelmed him with a deep sobbing and then after a time, sliding into integration, he felt a deep peace inside of him. The disappointment was gone and replaced by a love for himself and all life.

Opening his eyes, he looked again at the twelfth stone. Before his very eyes the understanding is there. He can read it. The words of Malkuth echoed in his head. "When you can read the twelfth stone, your next teacher will arrive. Be ready!'

**The Twelfth stone:
Be present. In you – all is.**

He nodded his understanding and smiled.

The End

Colin P. Sisson

Inspirational writer and speaker on the practice of being present, he has the unique ability to inspire the best in people. When people discover the present moment, not just as a theory, but as a practice of being here now, a gateway opens that leads directly into the reality of love, joy and inner freedom. All past suffering depression and trauma fall away, revealing the abundance and the excellence that are the basis of every human soul.

Colin was born in New Zealand and came a long way from being a country boy, prepared by his father for a career of a farmer, through the battlefields of Vietnam, and the trauma of post-war confusion

While struggling and fighting with life, he sought the answers to the eternal questions of humanity: the purpose of life, the reason for suffering, and the source of happiness. In his quest, he discovered many ways to expand awareness, and that wisdom is in simplicity and being here now. This led to the discovery of Breath Integration that eventually developed into Integrative Presence, the practice of being present.

His educational background is business law, economics, personal management and psychology. He, however, claims his greatest inspirations came from meditation, Qabalah studies, Zen, Taoism, yoga and the work of Gurdjieff. He is well known and respected for the contribution he made to rebirthing in 1985 world-wide through his bestselling book, Rebirthing Made Easy.

Colin's teachings are simple, practical, compassionate, and very powerful in their transforming results. His main principle is of inner-observation and self-responsibility. No teacher can do it for us, except the `teacher' within. Colin is a friend who assists us to discover this teacher.

Awarded `The Queen's Commendation for brave conduct', a civilian award, and is the author of ten books.

– Marina Kitchatova

Chapter Summary

Chapter   Page

1 **The Map**   1

Harold, a Vietnam veteran near retirement, finds a treasure map; the map is verified as genuine by the Museum of South American Ancient History; Jonathan, his son, agrees to accompany him to the Amazon jungle, where the treasure is buried.

2. **Beginning**   10

Their guide, Arizona, appears strange; they set off into the deep jungle of the Jaú National Park; over the first few days they cover much ground; the journey is becoming more difficult, but all appears to be going well.

3. **Harold's horror**   16

Jonathan adopts the two mules, Henry and Charlie, as pets; they discover a Goliath tarantula in their camp and it activates painful memories of Vietnam for Harold.

4. **River crossing**   22

Confronted by a huge river; an accident nearly caused Jonathan to drown; Jonathan's dead mother appears to him in the middle of his drowning crisis; half of their equipment is lost in the accident.

5. **The map's disappearance**   28
The shadowy figure; Arizona and the map disappear; Harold contemplates turning back, but Jonathan insists on going on; they prepare to pursue Arizona.

6. **Getting close**   35
Harold anguishes over possible armed conflict with Arizona; they find Arizona's trail; tragedy with one of the mules, Henry, but it shows them to the beacon and first clue to the treasure; the second clue is found as their excitement increases; the mystery deepens when Jonathan exclaims that the preceding events in the precise order they happened including the maps disappearance determined their success, otherwise they would never have found the clues; however, the last clue to finding the treasure eludes them.

7. **Treasure**   46
After much searching they at last find the final clue; the treasure is found but turns out to be different from what they expected; Jonathan is disgusted at finding a chest full of rocks; Harold's disappointment disappears when he discovers that each rock contains a hidden message that only he can read and feels that each rock contains a great ancient wisdom.

8. **Malkuth**   52
They set off back to civilization with the treasure of rocks; Harold suggests an army Special Forces trick to

put off a tracker if Arizona is pursuing them; Harold badly sprains his ankle while crossing a stream, preventing further travel for at least a week; intrigue deepens with a bright light signalling the arrival of a stranger called Malkuth; Malkuth offers Harold help in deciphering the meaning of the stones.

9. **Your search for truth will take you in the opposite direction**   63

Malkuth is more than mysterious, but friendly and helpful; Malkuth explains the history of the ancient stones and that they do contain a hidden message of great worth; together, Harold and Malkuth discuss a new approach to how the mind works and in doing so, unravel the secret of the first stone.

10. **See that you cannot see**   76

There is a violent storm; Jonathan comments on how young Harold looks after being in Malkuth's company; Harold reminisces about the special relationship he has with both his children, Marlene and Jonathan; the next morning Harold is astonished that there is no sign of the storm at Malkuth's camp; Malkuth introduces Harold to his own intuition that is beyond the intellect through being fully present; Harold discovers the secret of the second stone.

11. **Now is all there is, yet seek it not**   88

Harold starts his day feeling irritable for no apparent reason; his lack of understanding of the third stone spills over in his challenge to Malkuth; being present is expanded upon; Harold's numerous New Age workshops cause him much confusion about being present in the present moment; Malkuth encourages Harold to feel his feelings, to better connect with the present moment; Harold's irritation boils over as he connects with the grief of his wife, Helen, being killed in a motor accident ten years earlier and this brings him understanding of the third stone.

12. **Jungle life** 100

As the days pass, both Harold and Jonathan adopted to jungle life; luxury items are beginning to run out due to half their supplies being lost in the river incident; Harold shares with his son some lighter moments of his experiences in Vietnam; they exchange jokes, and a feeling of closeness surrounds father and son.

13. **The mind knows not itself** 107

Harold fails to understand the next stone; discussion with Malkuth centers around the three main functions: body, emotions and intellect; Malkuth introduces Harold to his own creativity and inspiration in connection with his intuition; Harold learns his first major exercise to becoming present; finally, Harold understands the fourth stone.

14. **What you value becomes your attachment and prison** 123

Harold practices being present with a headache and finds that it works; Harold discovers that he can understand the stones with small prompting from Malkuth; the limitation of values and purpose; the five attachments that limit experience in the present moment.

15. You are not who you think you are — 139
Marlene expresses her concern about their safety and Harold's fixation with positive thinking; personality leads to identification; identification with roles and functions stops us from being present; Harold judges himself that his thoughts still control him; nothing to change or give up, but transformation happens when we are present with an experience; confusion around the idea of the witness.

16. The unexpected — 151
Dragged from their beds by bandits; Jonathan concussed by a kick to the head by one of the intruders; Arizona is amongst them and questions Harold on the whereabouts of the treasure; not finding the expected treasure, the leader of the groups orders all their immediate execution, including Arizona; Malkuth suddenly arrives and from the power of his being causes the bandits to leave in peace after a dramatic confrontation between them; Arizona reveals some startling and mysterious information about Malkuth.

17. Beware of your benefactor — 163
Harold accuses Malkuth of being an enlightened master, which he denies, expressing the danger of spiritual hierarchy; unhealthy motivations in spiritual work; discussion about the master Christian; "If you meet the Buddha on the road, kill him"; Harold understands the seventh stone.

18. **Being and doing the two great powers that lead you home** 176

Jonathan feels he is watched; Harold discovers Malkuth's hidden cave; fear motivations appear in disguised ways; gender identification; the two great powers of doing and being; masculine and feminine thinking and feeling; society's conditioning causes imbalance; balance is restored through being present and results in creativity, inspiration and intuition.

19. **Alicia** 190

Jonathan sets a trap for the person spying on him; a teenage boy is caught, but immediately escapes; Jonathan chases the boy and finally catches up with him by persuading the youth that he is no threat; the boy turns out to be a beautiful young woman named Alicia; they become friends and set up a future meeting; Alicia disappears.

20. **The centre of your fear is a great power** 200

Love is real, fear is an illusion; the five attachments are the cause of fear; Harold reveals an experience from Vietnam that demonstrates the illusion of fear; escaping your fears is the greatest danger; Harold is confronted by his most terrifying fear.

21. **Jungle crisis** 213

Jonathan goes searching for Alicia. In his preoccupation, is bitten by a venomous snake far from any help. Malkuth feels his crisis and he and Harold go in search of him.

22. Being truthful to the moment — 220
Jonathan's life is threatened; Malkuth saves his life; a deep love has formed between Malkuth and Harold; making fear fully conscious transforms the illusion of love; dealing with overwhelming fears; the story of the white horse; going deeper into feelings; fighting, escaping and freezing our feelings in order not to feel them; the key questions to becoming free.

23. Alicia returns — 235
Alicia comes to their camp; she reveals her dark secret and family's plight; Jonathan and Alicia swim together and afterwards romantic feelings for each other are stirred.

24. Thought is a good servant and a poor master — 242
Harold feels he is regressing at his inability to understand the latest stone; perception and projections as people only see what they are trained or conditioned to see; thought is designed to be in the service of intuition; the pathless path of intuition is less popular than the well defined path of intellect; Eastern fable of heart and thought working together; intuition is the connecting link between our spiritual true self and our physical reality; defining rationality; intellectual and intuitive methods of gaining knowledge.

25. Know the two pathways home — 257
Two distinct paths to truth through learning and knowledge; activity; values; time; structure and essence;

direction and purpose; spirituality; being present connects you with who you are; know, feel and be it all.

26. Questions and answers — 267
Malkuth announces that tomorrow is their last meeting; a new teacher awaits Harold; instructions to reach his next teacher; the difference between awareness and knowing about; attachment and the 'just is' concept; aiming points; karma and parallel lives.

27 A chapter closes — 278
Clear differences between the two paths home; destiny of the world to eventually switch from the intellectual path to the pathless path of intuition; grieving of old ways; allowing intuition to exist, enables it; by being present with how you can't do something enables you to do it; taking spiritual life too seriously is another attachment.

28. The secret of the twelfth stone — 289
Harold remembers the previous day's highly emotional parting with Malkuth and the healing with his father; he revisits Malkuth's cave and makes a shocking discovery; Jonathan and Harold leave for his final mysterious meeting with Harold's next teacher who is to change his life forever; Harold confronts his last remaining fear through an encounter with a wild jaguar; his teacher fails to arrive, increasing Harold's doubts about not being able to read the twelfth stone; he asks the key question and is fully present; he finally understands the last stone and his most important teacher arrives.

www.ingramcontent.com/pod-product-compliance
Lightning Source LLC
Chambersburg PA
CBHW071649090426
42738CB00009B/1466